HEAVENS TO BETSY!

HEAVENS TO BETSY!

And Other Curious Sayings

CHARLES EARLE FUNK, Litt. D.

With Illustrations by TOM FUNK

HarperPerennial
A Division of HarperCollins*Publishers*

A hardcover edition of this book was published in 1955 by Harper & Row, Publishers, Inc.

HEAVENS TO BETSY! Copyright © 1955 by Charles Earle Funk. Copyright renewed © 1983 by Beulah M. Funk. All rights reserved. Printed in the United States of America. No part of this book may be used or reproduced in any manner whatsoever without written permission except in the case of brief quotations embodied in critical articles and reviews. For information address HarperCollins Publishers, Inc., 10 East 53rd Street, New York, NY 10022.

HarperCollins books may be purchased for educational, business, or sales promotional use. For information please write: Special Markets Department, HarperCollins Publishers, Inc., 10 East 53rd Street, New York, NY 10022.

First Perennial Library edition published 1986.

Reissued in HarperPerennial 1993.

Library of Congress Cataloging-in-Publication Data
Funk, Charles Earle, 1881-1957.
    Heavens to Betsy! and other curious sayings.
    "Perennial Library."
    1. English language—Terms and phrases.   2. English
language—Etymology.   I. Title.
PE1689.F757   1986   422   86-45102
ISBN 0-06-272011-2 (pbk.)

    99 00 01 RRD-H 30 29 28 27 26 25 24 23 22

TO MY WIFE

Who has most unmistakably been at my side "through sickness and health" during the preparation of this volume

FOREWORD

LONG BEFORE I began to prepare for publication the collection of sketches in the little volume, *A Hog on Ice and Other Curious Expressions,* brought out in 1948, I had been greatly interested in certain other sayings or expressions, equally curious, but about which I had not yet been able to learn anything. Why, for instance, did my father and others of his generation speak of Abraham Lincoln as a typical example of a man who had "lifted himself by his own bootstraps," or people of my own generation use the same saying of the Negro scientist, George Washington Carver? Why did my wife's father, a Massachusetts country doctor, so frequently during his lifetime say of a person who seemed uninterested in what was going on that he "just sat like a Stoughton bottle"? The reasons for these omissions I shall shortly explain.

There were, as well, a considerable number of other sayings, some in daily use and some that we encounter chiefly in literature, that justified further investigation or that I had omitted for one reason or another. And, to be frank about it, having no complete list of all the numerous sayings we employ in our speech, many did not occur to me at the time; interested readers of *A Hog on Ice* have subsequently called scores of them to my attention. In addition, in a few instances I have run across pertinent supplementary information about some expressions discussed in that book, usually through the courtesy of its readers, or, occasionally, I have wished to correct a statement or alter an opinion.

For these reasons, influenced also by the gratifying reception given to the earlier book, the publishers suggested that I prepare the present collection rather than to revise and greatly enlarge the former one. This I have done. The book stands alone, however;

its contents are independent of the previous book—at least, in the terms of a popular soap advertisement, "ninety-nine and 44/100 percent" independent. My nephew, Tom Funk, well known for his humorous drawings in many of our popular magazines, has again exercised his imagination in illustrating the text, which, I fear, is often in need of his lightsome aid.

The sayings that I have included owe their origins to all levels of life and take us back through virtually all periods of English and American history. A number had their origins in early translations of the Bible; others have come to us from the translations made in the classroom by ebullient young students of Greek and Latin in the days when those languages were an essential part of one's education. Many came from the everyday activities of men and women engaged in homely labor on the farm. Some are from the circus and the theater. Some are from the gambling table with cards or other games of chance. Some, chiefly used by political orators, are traceable to American frontier life. Many were undoubtedly slang expressions that were current at the period cited. Some— a very few, I've no doubt—were the carefully developed and deliberately phrased utterances of their creator.

The general formula that I have followed is that of the previous book—to give each curious saying the figurative meaning that it has acquired, to show, whenever possible, how that meaning came about, and to make an approximate estimate of the time it came into use in English speech, usually by quoting the one who, so far as records indicate, was the first to employ it in his writing. In such instances I have often gone back to the records themselves to summarize the occasion leading up to the writer's use of the expression, to say, for instance, why the diarist, Samuel Pepys, used the saying "to put one's nose out of joint," to relate the events leading up to Homer's use of "on the lap of the gods" in the *Iliad,* to give the circumstances that caused Mrs. Wiggs, in Alice Hegan Rice's *Mrs. Wiggs of the Cabbage Patch,* to say of her boarder that he was now "on the water-cart." Very rarely, of course, do I credit the actual coinage of these sayings to the writers quoted; with few exceptions, no doubt, these writers deserve nothing more than credit for passing along to posterity the popular sayings of their own day. We can no more determine who was the individual who first said that something was "as scarce as hen's teeth" than we can say with any certainty who, of modern times, was the first to say of some girl that she was "as cute as a bug's ear."

Who can predict what chance happy conversational phrasing may strike a listener as worthy of repetition? Who would think to record anywhere the original speaker? Who, not very long ago, first said of someone that he "took it on the lam"? who that so-and-so had "taken a powder"? Or, to go back a hundred and fifty years, what story brought into existence the metaphor, "Everyone to his taste, as the devil said when he painted his tail sky-blue"? Or to go back three hundred years, to the period of the English Protectorate, who had the happy thought to describe something as being "as tight as Dick's hatband"?

That is to say—or to confess—that very, very often in these pages I could do no more than to trace a saying back through the years or centuries to its earliest appearance in written literature, telling in the process any historical fact or other item of interest that might have a bearing on the origin. Thus, for example, though we know much of the legendary story of the medieval heroes, Roland and Oliver, it is little more than guesswork that can be offered to explain why "a Roland for an Oliver" means "tit for tat." Whenever possible, however, I have given exact sources of sayings that have come into common or literary use. It was the Cervantes hero, Don Quixote, who first "tilted at windmills"; it was the French poet, Sainte-Beuve, from whom we got our current meaning of an "ivory tower." Coming down to the present day, it was the comic-strip artist, Arthur ("Pop") Momand, who brought "Keeping up with the Joneses" into our popular speech, and his own story of its origin on pages 141 makes very interesting reading. So also does the account by Caswell Adams on page 197 telling how any of a certain group of Eastern colleges has come to be known as a member of the "Ivy League."

My search for sources of certain sayings, however, was attended by an inordinate amount of trouble, leading me at times into wholly unforeseen twists and turns. The title selected at the very outset for the book itself turned out eventually to be completely unsolvable. I am tempted to paraphrase Shakespeare: "Who is Betsy? what is she, That heaven itself commends her?" The exclamation is in daily use in all parts of the United States. Countless people, men and women—north, south, east, west—have said to me, "Why, I've used that all my life!" But not an inkling have I been able to find that would lead to a positive source. The expression, I am told, is not used in England, which eliminates any probability of connection with Queen Elizabeth of bygone years —known familiarly as "Bess" anyway, rather than "Betsy." Nor have I found any definite clue to the age of the saying. My friend, the historical novelist Kenneth Roberts, in one of his whimsical letters wrote:

I remember "Heavens to Betsy" from my earliest days in my grandmother's New Hampshire home—always spoken in a gently derisive sort of way, as was the remark, "Well, I snum!" . . . I think there's no doubt whatever that if I had sat down with her for an hour or so, I could have worked her around to hazarding a guess, and the guess would have run something like this: Our family originated in Auvergne, lit out when things were being made rough for Huguenots, settled in Salisbury, England, then in Godalming near Stratford-on-Avon. . . . I think there's no doubt that I could have persuaded her that "Heavens to Betsy" was nothing but a corruption of the words *Auvergne betisse,* meaning "What won't they think of next!" But she, alas, died fifty years ago.

Mr. Roberts fortified his belief in the age of the exclamation by an enclosed note from an elderly friend, Florence A. Redd, which read in part: "When I was about ten (I am now eighty-six) we had a hired girl whose favorite expression was 'Heavens to Betsy.' In fact she used it so often that we always referred to her as 'Heaven to Betsy.' " And in a subsequent note he called my attention to a passage on page 494 of his novel, *Oliver Wiswell,* in which Oliver, in 1777, says of the young Marquis de Lafayette, "He was the politest young man imaginable, and was forever smiling, kissing his finger tips to denote enthusiasm, or jumping from his chair to bow with his hand on his heart. I always knew when the little marquis arrived, because of Mrs. Byles' muffled artificial exclamations of 'Oh mercy me!' and 'Heavens to Betsy!' "

Well, though I don't doubt that "Heavens to Betsy!" is a hundred years old—it would almost have to be to have become so widespread before the days of rapid dissemination by radio, movies, or newspaper—I can't overlook the fact that *Oliver Wiswell* is fictional and was published no earlier than 1940. Possibly the phrase was known in Revolutionary War days, but I doubt it. Nor do I think, as some friends have suggested, that it pertained in any way to the maker of the first American flag, Betsy Ross. It is much more likely to have been derived in some way from the frontiersman's rifle or gun which, for unknown reason, he always fondly called Betsy. However, despite exhaustive search, I am reluctantly forced to resort to the familiar lexicographical locution, "Source unknown."

Almost as baffling was the saying we have used for generations, both in England and America, when speaking of (a) a person who, attempting the impossible, "might as well try to lift himself by the bootstraps," or (b) a person who, by determination and perseverance, laboring against almost impossible odds, succeeds in "raising himself by his bootstraps." Here I encountered the incredible fact that all dictionaries, from Randle Cotgrave's *Dictionarie of the French and English Tongues* of 1611 to and including the great *Oxford English Dictionary,* completed in 1933, had somehow managed to miss any definition of *bootstrap,* and that no dictionary nor other repository of idiomatic sayings contained any mention of this familiar phrase. Accordingly, as related in my discussion of the saying on page 51, the best that I have been able to do is to establish a fairly definite date before which the expression could not have existed.

But before I could establish even that time limit I was led into learning something of the history of boot-making, hence into consulting dozens of books and other references on boot- and shoe-making, as well as books on costume—none of which, incidentally, mentioned a bootstrap. Ultimately, as the most likely source for the information I sought, I wrote to the Northampton Town (England) Footwear Manufacturers' Association, representing the center of English boot- and shoe-making since the early seventeenth century. My inquiry was, to my good fortune, turned over to Mr. John H. Thornton, M.A., F.B.S.I., Head of the Department of Boot and Shoe Manufacture, Northampton College of Technology, a gentleman long interested in all phases of shoe history and a collector of historical items connected with the industry. The seventeenth-century Cromwellian boot, of which a sketch appears on page 51, is one of a pair from his collection. When worn by its original owner it had a spur held in place by a spur-leather over the instep, but these are missing. Heavy riding boots, according to Mr. Thornton, were the first to be made with bootstraps, and such boots did not come into use much before the end of the sixteenth century. The bootstrap, accordingly—or "strap," as then called—had not been known long when Shakespeare mentioned it in *Twelfth Night,* written in 1601.

The search for the mysterious Stoughton bottle, of the old New England saying, "to sit (or rarely, to stand) like a Stoughton bottle," which I had been quietly pursuing for a dozen years ultimately became fascinating and, I might say, fantastic. The definition given in *The New Standard Dictionary,* written in 1913 by some person unknown to me, reads:

Stoughton-bottle: A stupid person; figurehead; dolt; as, they stood there like stoughton-bottles: from the black or dark-green bottles of Dr. Stoughton's bitters, shaped like a log cabin and used in the Presidential campaign of 1840.

Though I had no material fault to find with the definition, I knew enough through hearsay and reading about the so-called "log cabin bottles" used in the wildly enthusiastic "Tippecanoe and Tyler, too" —William Henry Harrison and John Tyler—campaign of 1840 to mistrust the attached explanation. First, those bottles contained whisky (under the guise of hard cider, the only beverage, it was said, that Harrison knew in his youth). Second, and more decisive, just about every distiller in the country climbed aboard the band wagon by adopting for his product one or another bottle, colored or not, that somewhat resembled the appearance of a log cabin, the intent being to honor Harrison's alleged humble origin. That is to say, there was nothing so distinctive about one make of log-cabin bottle as to make it more doltish, more stupid in appearance than another.

The popularly called Webster Dictionary—*Webster's New International Dictionary, Second Edition,* by its full title—brought out in 1934, carried for the first time a definition of the bottle, thus:

Stoughton bottle. (After a Dr. Stoughton, the maker.) A bottle containing Stoughton's Elixir, a tincture of wormwood, germander, rhubarb, orange peel, cascarilla, and aloes, once widely used as a flavoring for alcoholic drinks and as a tonic.

to sit, stand, etc., *like a Stoughton bottle.* To sit, stand, etc., stolidly and dumbly.*

The inference is that "Dr. Stoughton" made the bottle as well as the elixir, though I doubt that such was the intent. However, no clue is offered as to why this particular bottle was so unique as to convey so definite an impression, nor why it must have been once so common that one hearing the phrase would immediately comprehend the meaning.

The Dictionary of Americanisms, published in 1951 by The University of Chicago Press, gave me no further information along those lines either, though its very friendly and helpful editor, Dr. Mitford M. Mathews, has written to say that "Stoughton bitters" received mention in American literature in 1847, ten years earlier than the date shown in his dictionary. Let me say here also, for the benefit of any doubting Thomas, one will find no further mention than I have given here of "Dr." Stoughton, Stoughton bitters or elixir, nor the Stoughton bottle in any encyclopedia or dictionary, American or English, not even in that monumental compendium of information, the *Oxford English Dictionary* nor its *Supplement.*

Now American bottle makers have turned out and are still turning out thousands of distinctive bottles, some so distinctive and familiar that, for example, any American traversing a hillside in Korea might point to a Coca-Cola bottle and say, "Well, I see I'm not the first American here." But in all our history the "Stoughton bottle" is the only one to have passed into a household expression. We can gather that it must have been squat in shape; that it must have appeared stolid; it must have looked stupid, or at least uncommunicative; it must have been fairly conspicuous; it certainly must have been a familiar object, and it must have been well known by name, especially in New England where the expression was best known.

Though the bottle described in the dictionary might conceivably meet some of those conditions—as also the two square bottles described in the book, *Bitters Bottles* by J. H. Thompson, published in 1947, early in my search—none met all. So I then began to inquire at every "antique shoppe" in which, on one pretext or another, we entered on our annual sojourns in New England, to make inquiries at New England museums, to make deliberate inquiry at country auctions, to hunt up people named Stoughton—a not uncommon patronym in New England. I drew nothing but blanks.

Eventually I sent letters telling of my search to several newspapers, and then began to get results—though not many, of course. My initial, and reasonable, assumption that the "Stoughton bottle" of the saying was glass was most obviously the opinion also of the majority of those who replied to my appeal, directly to me or through the newspapers—those who owned a bottle with the name "Stoughton" imprinted on its face or who owned a bottle which, by family tradition, was a "Stoughton bottle." Including those of which I had previous descriptions, I now had descriptions of eleven glass bottles—no two alike! Some letters were accompanied by sketches, of which six are shown here. The one in outline at the right was part of the following letter from the Bay State (name and address omitted):

Hi There—

Saw ad in Mass Papper where you Inquired about the Stoughton Bottel—That was an old whiskey Bottle Shaped like this [sketch] havent seen one in years will Enquire at Salem when get to town. That is this what you are looking for answer. That was made in New England glass works, not in Exsistence now. let me hear from you.

Sketches that contained dimensions showed the tallest bottle, the one of which only "ought" is visible, to be nine inches tall; the small pear-shaped bottle and the one shaped like a water carafe, each also bearing the name "Stoughton," were six and three-fourths and seven inches tall respectively.

Just possibly a person gifted with the imaginative powers of the Greek who named the heavenly constellations might be able to fit one or two of the necessary attributes to one or another of these bottles, but the very fact that there was such a variety made it impossible to accept any.

As I had been previously assured that the saying had never been known in England, I had also assumed that "Dr." Stoughton and his famous bitters were American, though the records of the United States Patent Office from 1790 to 1873 failed to indicate any patents to anyone named Stoughton for either bitters or bottle. My search was thrown into another direction at this point, in part from some other letters that replied to my newspaper inquiries, and in part from a statement made in an item in the "All Sorts" column of the Boston *Post,* conducted by Joe Harrington. Through subsequent correspondence with Mr. Harrington, the Library of the Boston Athenaeum, and the Carnegie Free Library of Allegheny (Pittsburgh), I now learned that the bitters—or more properly, elixir—contained in the mysterious bottle was a concoction of one Richard Stoughton, an apothecary of Southwark, London; that Stoughton began to publicize his "Great Cordial Elixir" in 1712—a century earlier than I had supposed—and that his preparation was the second medicine for which letters patent were granted in England, as stated in both *Chronicles of Pharmacy* by A. C. Wootton (1910, Macmillan, London) and *Four Thousand Years of Pharmacy* by C. H. LaWall (1927, Lippincott, Philadelphia). For other data concerning the elixir I am indebted to *The Quacks of Old London* by C. J. S. Thompson (1928, Brentano, London).

Stoughton's advertising bill makes various assertions as to the virtues and properties of his medicine, but the statement of interest to me was this: "The Elixir has twenty-two ingredients unknown to any one but me, and has now obtained a great reputation throughout England, Scotland, Ireland and the plantations beyond the Sea."

Well, I have no doubt that New England was included among "the plantations beyond the Sea." And I have no doubt further that so great were the real or acclaimed virtues of this elixir that shortly after the American colonies broke away from parent England, when "letters patent" were no longer a restraint, more than one American apothecary began to concoct his own version of this celebrated elixir.* They used such bottles as struck individual fancy. Some went so far as to have "Stoughton" impressed in the glass; others used printed labels. All retained the original maker's name, but though some may have sold their product as an "elixir," the more common American name appears to have been "Stoughton bitters." The use was primarily for flavoring an alcoholic beverage, though it was also sometimes recommended as a tonic. Quite likely also, some American distiller may have adopted the name and produced a "Stoughton whisky."

Some responses to my newspaper inquiries, however, directed my consideration into channels other than *glass* bottles. This part of the story is given more fully on page 33 in the discussion of "to sit (or stand) like a Stoughton bottle." The explanation necessarily involves a certain amount of deduction, because it may not now be possible to trace back to pre-Revolutionary times and determine the facts. That is, to a number of persons "Stoughton bottle" meant a kind of stoneware jug used—almost invariably—"in my boyhood (or girlhood) days by my grandmother as a bed-warmer." Inquiry among a number of my elderly acquaintances also now residing in Florida confirmed that statement. And, to my surprise, some of these of Canadian or English birth recalled a "Stoughton

* After this foreword was in type I received corroborative support for this surmise from Dr. Glenn Sonnedecker, Secretary, American Institute of the History of Pharmacy, whose letter says, in part: "There is evidence that 'Stoughton's Bitters' was being rather extensively used in the early 19th century. We have in our collection, for example, a manuscript 'Order Book' of a Philadelphia wholesale druggist—probably Jeremiah Emlen. This shows a number of entries during 1815 and 1816 for sales of 1 to 5 dozen 'Stoughton's Bitters,' at $1.25 per dozen (size of unit unspecified)."

A later letter from Dr. Sonnedecker adds further support. He says: " 'Stoughton's Elixer [sic] Magnum Stomachicum' is listed in the *Catalogue of Drugs and Medicines* [etc.], *imported, prepared, and sold by Smith and Bartlett, at their Druggists Store and Apothecaries Shop, No. 61, Cornhill, Boston,* Manning and Loring, Boston, 1795, p. 18."

bottle" put to the same use in their childhood days. This confirmed a letter from a New England nurse who said that in her probationary days in a London hospital forty-odd years ago her early duty had been to fill some thirty "Stoughton bottles" three or four times a day as foot warmers for the patients.

It is my belief, therefore, though I cannot prove it, that for safety in transportation "throughout England, Scotland, Ireland, and the plantations beyond the Sea," the Great Cordial Elixir concocted by Richard Stoughton was shipped in stoneware containers or "bottles" which, because of convenient size and heat-retaining qualities, were prized by grandmother's great-grandmother and, when empty, were filled with hot water on cold winter nights and used as foot warmers in bed or in a sleigh, and in summer were filled with sand and used as doorstops. In shape, appearance, conspicuousness, and familiarity the year around these distinctive bottles, of which several designs are shown on page 36, fulfil all the requirements.

The works that I have consulted, often futilely, in the preparation of these "where we got it" sketches would run into many hundreds, if I were able to list them. They would embrace the dictionaries of many languages, encyclopedias, volumes on customs and fashions of bygone generations—Greek, Roman, English, American. They would include histories of England and America, and the biographies of many men. Dictionaries of slang have been helpful—American, by Berrey and Van den Bark; English, by Partridge, as well as Farmer, and older works. But the collection could not have been presented in the manner chosen had it not been for the excellent research material available in the *Oxford English Dictionary on Historical Principles* and its *Supplement,* the *Dictionary of American English* and the more recent *Dictionary of Americanisms,* both of which are also on historical principles. To the editor of the last-named tome, Dr. Mitford M. Mathews, I am especially indebted for his ready response to numerous requests. For assistance from England in times of need I owe thanks in particular to Sir St. Vincent Troubridge, whose name will be found more than once in the following pages, and to Ivor Brown, whose books, *A Word in Your Ear* and *Just Another Word,* have delighted many readers. I am indebted also to various other individuals in both countries for aid on one or another single item, and I have been impressed repeatedly by the willingness of librarians in my peregrinations north and south to offer suggestions and dig out musty references—Springfield (Vermont), Dartmouth University, New York Public Library, University of North Carolina, University of Florida, Mount Dora (Florida), and especially Maureen J. Harris of the Alderson Library, Orlando, Florida.

CHARLES EARLE FUNK

Mount Plymouth, Florida
March, 1955

xviii

HEAVENS TO BETSY!

to play cat and mouse with one

Everyone has seen the way a cat acts with a mouse that she has caught. The poor little animal, half dead with fright or injury, waits with beating heart until the cat has apparently forgotten it or gone to sleep, and then may get halfway to its hole or other place of safety, only to be pounced upon and again tossed around. Figuratively, then, when sweet and capricious Susan "plays cat and mouse" with lovesick Peter, she is by turns seemingly indifferent to him or mercilessly possessive if he dare cast an eye at another maid. She has him on a string. The expression came into popular use in England in 1913 during the suffragette agitation.  Women, arrested for disturbing the peace, resorted to the hunger strike, thus endangering health. To get around such voluntary martyrdom Parliament passed an act called the "Prisoners' Temporary-Discharge-for-Ill-Health Act," which promptly became known as the "Cat-and-Mouse Act." Namely, it provided that a hunger striker could be released, but was subject to re-arrest to serve out the remainder of a sentence whenever danger to health was removed.

at the eleventh hour

With not a moment to spare; at the latest time possible; just under the wire. This is of Biblical origin, Matthew xx,1–16: "For the kingdom of heaven is like unto a householder, which went out early in the morning to hire labourers into his vineyard. And when he had agreed with the labourers for a penny a day, he sent them into his vineyard. . . . And about the eleventh hour he went out and found others standing idle, and saith unto them, Why stand ye here all the day idle? They say unto him, Because no man hath hired us. He saith unto them, Go ye also into the vineyard; and whatsoever is right, that shall ye receive." But at evening all received the same payment. Despite the protests of those who had "borne the burden and heat of the day," those who came at the eleventh hour received a penny, just as those who had come early in the morning.

a tempest in a teacup

Of course, the old Romans had neither teacup nor tea, but they did have a saying so like ours as to be usually translated in our wording: *excitare fluctus in simpulo*. The literal meaning is "to stir up a tempest in a small ladle"; hence, to storm about over trifles, to make much ado about nothing. In our literature the "teacup" analogy did not appear before 1872, but as long ago as 1678 small affairs were compared with great affairs as "but a storm in a cream bowl," and, in 1830, as "a storm in a wash-basin."

for crying out loud

An ejaculation, usually indicating complaint or astonishment; as, "For crying out loud, why did you do a thing like that?" Many of the users of this expression would be shocked to learn that it is in the category known as a minced oath; that is, a substitute based on, but slightly differing from a profanity. The expression is a high-school adaptation of about twenty-five years' standing of the profane ejaculation, "for Christ's sake."

a rift in the lute

It is the poet, Alfred Lord Tennyson, to whom we are indebted for this saying, and he expressed its meaning in the lines from *The Idylls of the King* (Merlin and Vivien, 1870) in which it appeared:

> Faith and unfaith can ne'er be equal powers:
> Unfaith in aught is want of faith in all.
> It is the little rift within the lute,
> That by and by will make the music mute,
> And ever widening slowly silence all.

a hair of the dog that bit you

This stems from the ancient medical maxim, Like cures like—
Similia similibus curantur. Thus, even in the *Iliad* we find the Greek
belief that a wound caused by the spear of Achilles could be healed
by an ointment containing rust from that same spear. And to this
day there are men and women who sin-
cerely believe that the best cure from the
bite of a dog is some of the hair from that
dog applied to the wound. In England,
they say, the hair should be burned before
it is applied. But, generally speaking, when
men get together, "a hair of the dog that
bit you" means another little drink. If the
conviviality of last night's sessions has resulted in a morning's hangover, the "hair"

is supposed to be a pick-me-up, a little whisky to clear the head.
This was the meaning among gentlemen four hundred years ago, as
recorded in John Heywood's *Prouerbes in the Englishe Tongue*
(1546): "I pray the leat me and my felow haue / A heare of the
dog that bote us last night."

in the dumps

Feeling blue; depressed; dejected; low in spirits. People felt this
way and so expressed themselves four hundred years ago, though no
one knew then (or now, for that matter) just what "dumps" meant.
Sir Thomas More, in *A Dialoge of Comforte against Tribulation*
(1534), has: "What heapes of heauynesse [heaviness], hathe of
late fallen amonge vs alreadye, with whiche some of our poore
familye bee fallen in suche dumpes."

to strike while the iron is hot

To act at the most fitting moment; to seize the most favorable
opportunity. It was, of course, the blacksmith who was originally
so exhorted. If he failed to swing his hammer while the metal on
the anvil was still glowing, nothing would do but to start up the
forge again and reheat the iron. His time was lost; the opportunity

for effective work had passed. Figurative use is very old. It is found in Chaucer's *Canterbury Tales,* "The Tale of Melibeus," (1386): "Right so as whil that Iren is hoot men sholden smyte."

A-number-one (A No. 1)

Superior, first class, the best of its kind. An American nautical classification of British ancestry, both of which referred originally to sailing vessels. The British term, usually written "A 1," was thus described in Lloyd's Register: "The character A denotes new ships, or ships renewed or restored. The stores of vessels are designated by the figures 1 and 2; signifying that the vessel is well and sufficiently found." The American term had a slightly different sense, as described in *Goodrich's Fifth School Reader* (1857): "Vessels are classified according to their age, strength, and other qualities. The best class is called A, and No. 1 implies that the Swiftsure stands at the head of the best class of vessels."

Charles Dickens was the earliest writer to give the British phrase a non-nautical use. In *Pickwick Papers* (1837), the faithful valet, Sam Weller, wants to know what kind of "gen'l'men" already occupy the prison room in which Mr. Pickwick is to be confined. The turnkey, Roker, describes one who "takes his twelve pints of ale a-day, and never leaves off smoking even at his meals." "He must be a first-rater," says Sam. "A-1," Roker answered.

And Harriet Beecher Stowe, in *Dred, A Tale of the Great Dismal Swamp* (1856), has the distinction of being the first to introduce the American phrase into literary use. She has Father Bennie, the preacher who buys and sells slaves as a sideline, ask a dealer, "You got a good cook in your lot, hey?" "Got a prime one," the dealer answered, "an A number one cook, and no mistake."

a bone to pick

A difficulty to be solved; a nut to be cracked; a complaint, dispute, misunderstanding or the like to be settled. The original idea was something to mull over or to occupy one as a bone occupies a dog. The Germans had the same idea but used a different simile, *ein Hünchen zu pflücken,* a bird to pluck; the French said, *une maille à partir,* a knot to pick; and in ancient Rome it was *scrupulum alicui injicere,* a pebble to throw.

An anonymous newspaper columnist recently said that this expression "started in Sicily where the father of a bride would give the bridegroom a bone to pick clean of meat as a symbol of the difficult task of marriage that he was undertaking." His statement of the Sicilian custom may be true, but any connection between that custom and our English expression of more than four hundred years is beyond credibility.

The related expression that we use commonly nowadays—"to have a bone to pick with one," to have a complaint to settle with one—is much more recent, dating back scarcely a hundred years.

to crack a crib

This is not modern slang. In the cant of thieves, "crack" has meant "to break open" since the early eighteenth century or earlier, and "crib," meaning "a house, shop," was known to Charles Dickens when he wrote *Oliver Twist* in 1838, and was used by the underworld thirty years or more before that date. Henry Kingsley used the full expression in the novel, *Ravenshoe,* in 1861.

rich as Croesus

Croesus succeeded his father and became king of Lydia, a country of Asia Minor, in 560 B.C. Through successive wars he greatly increased his dominions and, by such means and through trade within his own realm and with neighboring kingdoms, he became enormously wealthy. Probably his wealth was not actually as great as it was reputed, for the figures were fabulous. It became proverbial in his day, and is still used metaphorically as denoting great wealth. He died, however, in 546 B.C., after his kingdom had been overcome by Cyrus.

skeleton at the feast

An element of gloom or depression; an omen of misfortune; a reminder of possible disaster in the midst of pleasure. The allusion is to a custom in ancient Egypt as related by Plutarch (*c.* A.D. 46 to 120) in his *Moralia.* He tells us that at the conclusion of a feast a household servant carried a mummy into the banquet hall as a reminder to the guests that all men are mortal. However, our present phrase did not arise in English literature before the middle of the nineteenth century. It is best known, perhaps, from Longfellow's "The Old Clock on the Stairs," stanza 5:

> In that mansion used to be
> Free-hearted Hospitality;
> His great fires up the chimney roared;
> The stranger feasted at his board;
> But, like the skeleton at the feast,
> That warning timepiece never ceased,—
> "Forever—never!
> Never—forever!"

to take under one's wings

"O Jerusalem, Jerusalem, thou that killest the prophets, and stonest them which are sent unto thee, how often would I have gathered thy children together, even as a hen gathereth her chickens under her wings, and ye would not!" This passage from Matthew  xxiii, 37, was the source of our present expression. The metaphorical protection like that of a mother bird over her young appears also in Psalms lxiii, 7—"Because thou hast been my help, therefore in the shadow of thy wings will I rejoice." However, some of us may be more familiar with the saying from the lines of the Gilbert & Sullivan operetta, *The Mikado,* sung by Ko-Ko:

> The flowers that bloom in the spring,
>   Tra la,
> Have nothing to do with the case.
> I've got to take under my wing,
>   Tra la,
> A most unattractive old thing,
>   Tra la,
> With a caricature of a face.

one's cake is dough

One's plans have miscarried; one is disappointed. The proverb was old in the time of Shakespeare. In *Taming of the Shrew*, Act I, scene 1, he has Gremio saying to Hortensio, both suitors of Bianca, "Their love is not so great, Hortensio, but we may blow our nails together, and fast it fairly out; our cake's dough on both sides." Apperson reports the occurrence of the expression in the *Prayers* of Thomas Becon, 1559: "Or else your cake is dough, and all your fat lie in the fire." The allusion is obvious: when an oven does not reach a baking heat, one's plans for a cake have miscarried.

to speak by the card

The sense of this is nicely shown by Shakespeare's use of it in *Hamlet*. There, in Act V, scene 1, he has Hamlet himself use it in his conversation with the grave-digging clown who takes everything that Hamlet says in its most literal meaning. Finally Hamlet turns to his friend, Horatio, and says: "How absolute the knave is! we must speak by the card, or equivocation will undo us." He realized, that is, that he would have to express himself precisely, or he would get some such answer as Gracie Allen gives when she takes any remark literally. Shakespeare, the first on record to use the expression, undoubtedly alluded to the mariner's card, which may have been either the sea-chart or card, the nautical map indicating the position of rocks, sandbars, capes, and so on along a coast, or the circular card of stiff paper with the points of the compass upon it. In either case, "by the card" would denote absolute precision.

to call the turn

Let's quote some passages from Hoyle's rules for the game of faro: "The cards are shuffled and placed in a dealing box, from which they can be withdrawn only one at a time. . . . The dealer pulls out two cards, one at a time, the first card being laid aside, the one under it being placed close to the box; and the next one left showing. . . . The banker pays even money on all bets but the last turn. When only three cards remain, all different, they must come in one of six ways and the bank pays four for one if the player can call the turn. . . ." Thus, you see, if one can guess correctly, in the game of faro, how the last three cards will appear, or if one can guess correctly how any transaction or affair will develop, he "calls the turn."

to chew the fat (or rag)

Back in the fourteenth century, in Wyclif's time, they "chewed the cud"—and we still do, in imitation of the reflective appearance of cows as they lie patiently working their jaws. But to chew the fat, or rag, does not necessarily involve meditation; it usually involves nothing more than working the jaws in complaint, disputation, idle speech, vain argument, or just gossip. "Rag (or fat) chewing" we have had since the early 1880's. It was then classed as American Army slang, in Patterson's *Life in the Ranks*. To my notion, although either expression may have been adopted into army lingo, both are much more likely to have alluded to ladies' sewing circles—to the "rags," or cloth, upon which they worked while tongues clattered, or to the "fat," or choice morsels of gossip, upon which they could feast.

to cash in (hand in, or pass in) one's checks (or chips)

Whichever the phraseology, it adds up to the one result—to die. The allusion is to the American game of poker, in which a player may at any time drop from the game and turn in (hand in, or pass in) his chips or checks to the banker in exchange for cash. Perhaps on some few occasions, in the wild and woolly West, a man withdrew from an unfinished game only on pain of death, but our metaphorical usage had no such sinister general meaning at the time of its birth.

Charley-horse

A paragrapher in *Ladies' Home Journal* (Vol. LXX, No. 12) asserted without hesitation that this term for muscular stiffness came about thus: In the 1890's, a horse (named Charley) which drew a roller in the White Sox ball park in Chicago had a peculiar limp. Hence, the fans applied the name "Charley-horse" to any player afflicted with a muscular stiffness or lameness.

I can't deny that there may have been such a horse; however, if so, he must have performed his duties and to have had his name applied to such an injury some time before the 1890's. The term was used by a Cincinnati paper early in 1889, telling why a ball-player had withdrawn from the game in 1888, and inasmuch as the nature of the injury was not described, it is obvious that "Charley-horse" was well understood by baseball fans, at least, even outside of Chicago, before this latter date. Regrettably, we must continue to say "Origin unknown," despite much and varied speculation.

white-collar worker

Anyone who performs non-manual labor; a professional person, such as lawyer, doctor, banker, clergyman, etc.; specifically, an office worker, rather than a shop worker. An anonymous newspaper columnist recently stated that the expression started "when medicine became a respected profession and doctors began to wear white collars as part of their uniforms." The statement is an absurdity on the face of it. Medicine was "a respected profession" in the time of Galen and, though it may have fallen into some disrepute in the Middle Ages, it has certainly regained respect since the seventeenth century, long before the era of the white collar. Actually the label is recent and wholly unrelated to medicine or to uniforms of any sort. Originally it was the counterpart of the British "black-coated worker," a clerical employee, that is. The term originated during World War I.

the admirable Crichton

There was actually an individual who was so called, though not during his brief life. His real name was James Crichton, a son of Robert Crichton, lord advocate of Scotland. He is believed to have been born in 1560, and to have died at the early age of twenty-two, but his learning and athletic attainments were most remarkable—if the reports of Sir Thomas Urquhart and Aldus Manutius are to be credited. Urquhart, who wrote seventy years after Crichton's death, says that he held a dispute one time in the college of Navarre in twelve languages, and the next day won a tilting match. Aldus, who was a contemporary, is slightly more modest in his claims for his hero, but says that he spoke ten languages, could compose

Latin verse on any subject, was a mathematician and theologist, was extravagantly handsome and with the bearing of a soldier. The epithet, "the Admirable Crichton," was applied by John Johnston in his *Heroes Scoti* (1603), and is now sometimes bestowed upon any man of unusual grace and superior accomplishments.

to make no bones about (a matter)

To speak frankly; to come out flat-footed; to talk straight from the shoulder; hence, to have no scruples; to show no reluctance, also, to make no mistake (about it), to count on (it). *The Paston Letters* (1459) contain the line, "And fond [found] that tyme no bonys in the matere," and the poet, John Skelton, in *The Tunnyng of Elynour Rummyng* (1529), wrote, "She founde therein no bones," wherein in each case "to find no bones" was equivalent to "to find no difficulty; to have no hesitation." Accordingly, it seems evident that the allusion in the earliest form of our present expression was to the actual occurrence of bones in stews or soup; "no bones" would be indicative of no difficulty or no hesitation in the swallowing. The change to today's expression is shown in the translation by Nicholas Udall (1548) of *Erasmus's Paraphrase of Luke:* "He made no manier bones ne stickyng [no scruples nor hesitation], but went in hande to offer up his only son Isaac." Many writers since that date have "made no bones" about employing the phrase.

cheek by jowl

In early usage, six hundred years ago, when anyone wanted to express close intimacy, he said (or wrote), "cheke bi cheke." But some two centuries later someone thought it would be more picturesque to substitute the Frenchified "jowl"—variously written *jowl, joul, joll, jole, geoul, chowl*—for the second element, and this has been our choice ever since. It still means "cheek by cheek."

cute as a bug's ear

On the theory that the smaller they come the cuter they are, this modern American metaphor epitomizes the acme of cuteness, for if a small ear is cute, the ear of a bug—if bugs have ears—must be the cutest thing imaginable. Sometimes the expression is paraphrased into "cute as a bug in a rug," but this is a poor foist of new upon old. "Snug as a bug in a rug," the utmost in contentment and comfort, dates back two hundred years.

to lead by the nose

To dominate; to have control over; to have the whip hand or under one's thumb; to hold under submission. The expression is a common one in European languages, and both Romans and Greeks of old "had a word for it." The allusion is obvious: From the time  when beasts of burden were first domesticated, even as the oxen of the present time, it was found that they could be controlled and led by chain or cord attached to a ring through the septum of the nose. In the Roman Circus, trainers of wild animals sometimes thus led beasts that they had captured around the arena. Through the Middle Ages and even to recent times, bears have been so displayed. For Biblical reference we have Isaiah xxxvii, 29: "Because thy rage against me, and thy tumult, is come up into mine ears, therefore will I put my hook in thy nose, and my bridle in thy lips, and I will turn thee back by the way by which thou camest."

to know chalk from cheese

There was a time when coloring matter was not used in the making of cheese. Consequently, chalk and cheese were of the same whiteness. Such, at least, was the state of affairs in the fourteenth century. Perhaps, too, an unscrupulous tradesman would now and then take advantage of an innocent young housewife and sell her a piece of chalk which he had carefully shaped to resemble a cheese. At any rate, comparisons of chalk with cheese began to crop up at every opportunity. John Gower, in *Confessio Amantis* (1590), wrote, "Lo, how they feignen [counterfeit] chalk for chese." Such comparisons carry on to the present time from habit, though for several centuries the two substances no longer have had even a superficial resemblance.

to back and fill

To shilly-shally; to be vacillating or irresolute; to assert and deny, hem and haw; not to know if one is on one's head or heels. Originally this was said of ships, of sailing ships especially, attempting to negotiate a narrow channel when wind and tide were adverse and there was no room for tacking. Under such conditions a vessel may be worked to windward by keeping it broadside on to the current in mid-channel by counter-bracing the yards or keeping the sails shivering—that is, alternately backing and filling the sails. The progress of the ship is thus alternately backward and forward, in herringbone pattern; hence, anything that appears to do nothing more than to recede and advance, to vacillate, is said to back and fill.

between the devil and the deep blue sea

On the horns of a dilemma; between equally perilous dangers. I was reminded by a correspondent (whose signature, regrettably, I have been unable to decipher) that I had not gone far enough in my discussion of this expression in *A Hog on Ice*. "Devil," in this phrase—as also in "the devil to pay"—is a nautical term. In the days when hulls were of wooden construction, the term was applied to a seam between two planks which, because of its location or of its length, was especially accursed by sailors. In this instance, "devil" probably referred to the seam on a ship's deck nearest the side; hence, the longest seam on the deck, extending on a curve from stem to stern, and, from its location, a most dangerous one to calk or fill with pitch. Anyone between the devil and the deep (blue) sea had a very narrow footing, a narrow margin for choice.

"Devil" was also applied to the seam that was at, or just above, the water line of a ship's hull. Here again space was narrow and the margin of safety was negligible.

not worth a hill of beans

Beans, like straw, have long indicated small value. "Not to care a straw" means that the speaker has little more than the slightest concern over that of which he speaks, no more than the value of the straw trampled upon by householders of old. And the bean has long had no higher regard. ("Hill" is American hyperbole, inserted about a hundred years ago for exaggerated emphasis.) The expression is one of the oldest in the language. We find it used by Robert of Gloucester back in 1297 in his *English Chronicles,* page 497:

> þe king of alimayne sende specialliche inou
> To king Ion þat he wiþdrowe him of is wou
> & vnderuenge þe erchebissop & holichurche al clene
> Lete abbe ir franchise & al nas wurþ a bene.

We don't speak or write that way now, thank heavens, but freely translated it reads: "The king of Almain [Germany] sent [a message] especially to king John to forget his hurt, and receive the archbishop, and let Holy Church have her franchise, clear and clean; altogether not worth a bean."

to sit (or stand) like a Stoughton bottle

To sit (or stand) dumbly apathetic, stolidly, without expression, stupidly, like a bump on a log. I know well its meaning, as my wife's father, a New England country doctor, used it frequently during his lifetime in referring to anyone, member of his family or not, who appeared to be thus blankly uninterested in whatever was being said or done. Furthermore, the expression has been defined similarly in the *Funk & Wagnalls New Standard Dictionary* since 1913 and in the *Merriam-Webster New International Dictionary* since 1934. But it did not occur to me to ask my father-in-law, until too late, why a Stoughton bottle—presumably a bottle containing a tonic or bitters originally compounded at some undetermined time by a "Dr." Stoughton—acquired such a metaphorical meaning.

The lengthy search for a bottle, which by dictionary account was of glass, that would meet the conditions indicated by the figurative meaning is related in the foreword. It entailed much correspondence. The mysterious "Dr. Stoughton" turned out to be an English apothecary of Southwark, London. I had been seeking an American; our metaphor is of New England origin, wholly unknown in England. Stoughton's compound was the second medicine to be granted "letters patent" in England. That was in 1712, a hundred years earlier than I had supposed. Its full name was Stoughton's Great Cordial Elixir. In the early advertisements, according to *The Quacks of Old London* (1928), by C. J. S. Thompson, to which I owe this information in part, this elixir was a remedy "for all distempers of the stomach"; fifty or sixty drops of it "more or less as you please" were recommended to be taken "as often as you please" in a glass of "Spring water, Beer, Ale, Mum, Canary, White wine, with or without sugar, and a dram of brandy." (Can you not see how our great-great-grandsires would welcome this tonic for "distempers of the stomach"?)

The prospective purchaser was further told: " 'Tis most excellent in Tea, in Wine, very pleasant and proper, and in Beer or Ale, makes the best Purl in the world, and Purl Royal in Sack, giving all of them a fragrant smell and taste, far exceeding Purl made with wormwood and now used to drink in their wine at Taverns." (Purl was a spiced malt beverage popular at that period.) Then Stoughton added, the elixir "has now obtained a great reputation throughout England, Scotland, Ireland and the plantations beyond the Sea," and he concluded his bill with the offer, "If any Captain or Seaman, Book-seller, Stationer, Coffee-man, or any keeping a Publick House, wants any quantities to dispose of or sell again, they may be furnished with good allowance by letter or otherwise."

It would appear that New England was one "plantation beyond the Sea" where Stoughton's elixir had "obtained a great reputation," and that some unknown Captain, Seaman, or, most likely, a keeper of a "Publick House" profited favorably from its importation and resale. But it is not remotely probable that glass bottles of any size, nature, or description were used in the eighteenth century for shipping this liquid, either by sailing vessels or by carts that may have carried it throughout England and Scotland. On the contrary, it is almost certain that the bottles were glazed earthen- or stoneware, of the same nature as the pottery bottles in which

Holland gin has been shipped until recent years. And just as these latter bottles are spoken of as "Holland gin bottles" because of the original contents, so must the older bottles have been known as "Stoughton bottles."

I do not know either the shape or the size of those eighteenth-century bottles nor whether any may have been preserved in any collection of ceramics. But they were evidently of sufficient size to justify the housewife or grandmother in saving them when empty. In the unheated bedrooms of both England and America they made excellent foot warmers, when filled with hot water and stoppered well. And in summer, filled with sand, they were again useful as doorstops. In one capacity or another a Stoughton bottle was always in evidence. Even when not in use it probably stood in a corner somewhere, and it is likely that the housewife had several of them. It never talked back nor participated in any activity. Whether standing on its unglazed end or lying (sitting) on its side it was expressionless, stupid, apathetic.

It may be that production and importation of the famous elixir died with Richard Stoughton—the twenty-two ingredients, according to his advertisement, were unknown to anyone but him. Or it may have been that events following the Revolutionary War shut off its importation. But so persistent was the repute of this elixir that an American product, under the general name "Stoughton bitters," began to appear, probably about the turn of the century. And as neither the name nor the ingredients were now protected, I have no doubt that several makers produced their own versions of the compound and put them on sale in glass bottles of their own selection, thus accounting for the wide variety of bottles described in the foreword.

Moreover, the stoneware bottles also ceased to arrive from England. However, that was not long a matter of concern. American potteries began to supply that want of the housewife and to turn out foot warmers of better design—and these, because of long association, were still called Stoughton bottles. I do not know to what extent these American "bottles" may have differed from those that formerly had come from England. Of the first two shown in the accompanying illustration, the one on the left, bearing no label nor maker's name, was lent to me by its present owner, Mrs. Elizabeth H. Brown of Vermont, who, after purchasing it at an auction, was told by a nurse that it was a Stoughton bottle. From the evidence of other letters and various persons to whom I have shown it, I think bottles of this type were the more common. Note the broad flanges on the lower side to check the bottle from rolling, also the firm base on which it may be stood. The bottle in the center, with decorations baked in, labeled "Boss Foot Warmer" and

made in Portland, Maine, was presented to me by Kenneth Roberts and comes from other ancestral relics in the cellar of his home in Maine. The stopper, also stoneware, screws into the filler opening upon a rubber washer. The third bottle, of which detail drawings were sent to me by Russell Thornquist of Palmer, Massachusetts, whose sister owns it, was made or sold by P. L. Pride, Worcester, Massachusetts, and is of unusual design, as shown by the right-hand sketch. This bottle, also known as a Stoughton bottle, may be called a modern version, for it was purchased for use in the Rutland, Massachusetts, sanitarium as recently as 1926. Each of these three bottles is eleven or twelve inches in length and fifteen inches in circumference. The knob at the end of each was for convenience in lifting or carrying. A fourth bottle, which its present owner says was just called a hot-water jug, but does not describe, was made, according to imprint, by "Dorchester Pottery W'ks, Boston." A fifth one, described only from girlhood recollections, was said to have been twenty-four inches long, though only fifteen inches in circumference, resembling "a very large piece of bologna."

I have not been able to obtain a description of the Stoughton bottles which, until recent years at least, were in use in England. Information concerning use there is from isolated sources—Yorkshire, Northumberland, London—but details are lacking.

Incidentally, if the reader is seized with an urge to own a Stoughton bottle, he stands a better chance of success if, in browsing around a New England antique store, he asks the dealer if he happens to have a stoneware "pig."

to give (or get) the third degree

One who is a member of a Lodge of Freemasons knows so well the original meaning of this common expression that he will see little occasion for its inclusion here. But there are many who use it freely, however, who suppose it to have some connection with criminal law. Thus, in the United States, a murder that is deliberate is called murder in the first degree; one that is unintentional is murder in the second degree. Wrongly, therefore, it is supposed that some form of crime is in the third degree.

Actually the term "third degree" has no connection with criminality or brutal treatment or mental torture. It refers to the third and final stage of proficiency demanded of one who seeks to become a Master Mason. In each of the two preceding stages or degrees certain tests of proficiency are required, but before the candidate is fully qualified for the third degree he must undergo a very elaborate and severe test of ability, not even faintly injurious, physically or mentally. It is from this examinaton that "third degree" became applied to the treatment of prisoners by the police, and it was through the fact that the police sometimes did employ brutality in efforts to extort confession or information that our present expression obtained its common modern meaning.

dark and bloody ground

A title sometimes given to the state of Kentucky, so called because of the numerous raids by Indians upon white settlers in the early days of colonization. Very little was known about the region before 1752, and the first white colony was not established until 1774, at Harrodsburg. Few Indians, mainly Chickasaws near the Mississippi, inhabited the region, but it was claimed as hunting grounds by tribes from Tennessee and from southern Ohio. Despite treaties, therefore, bands of Indians would descend upon isolated farms or even villages to kill and burn. This was especially true under British instigation during the Revolutionary War, when the settlers were neglected by Virginia, in whose territory the country then lay, and were compelled to attempt to defend themselves. John Filson was the first to record the title in his history, *Kentucke* (1784): "The fertile region, now called Kentucke, then but known to the Indians, by the name of the Dark and Bloody Ground, and sometimes the Middle Ground." Filson erred on his translation, however, though the true meaning of the Indian name, Kentucky, is still not positively known.

to be caught flat-footed

In American usage, one is "caught flat-footed" when he is unprepared, asleep at the switch, inattentive, or surprised. In *A Hog on Ice,* page 57, I said that the expression probably arose from the American game of football, "for it applies most pertinently to the player who, having received the ball on a pass, is caught by an opposing player before he has moved from his tracks." My friend, Sir St. Vincent Troubridge, insists, "This is without doubt at all from horse-racing, quite solidly established in this country [England] from the reign of Queen Anne." In further correspondence he added: "In this country horse races are not started from stalls as ·with you, but by the horses advancing in line to a 'gate,' or barrier of tapes and webbing, which is raised by the starter by means of a lever when he is satisfied that the horses are in line. It will be clear that any horse which is 'caught flat-footed'—i.e., with all four feet on the ground, instead of dancing forward on his toes, so to speak, when the 'gate' rises—is at a disadvantage and will lose many lengths at the start. *Mutatis mutandis* the same would apply to men at the start of a foot-race, who are normally right forward on their toes awaiting the pistol shot."

dead as a herring

Very, very dead. Any dead fish soon acquires an exceedingly ancient odor if left exposed for only a few hours, but the odor of a dead herring becomes twice as noticeable. That is the reason herrings are used, by dragging them over a trail, in the teaching of young dogs to follow a scent. The expression probably started as a

variation of "dead as a doornail" (see *A Hog on Ice*, page 195)
back in the sixteenth century. Shakespeare used both. He put the
present one into the mouth of Doctor Caius, in *Merry Wives of
Windsor*, Act II, scene 3. Jealous of the curate, Sir Hugh Evans,
who also seeks the hand of Mistress Anne Page, Caius threatens to
kill him in a duel, which the two parties, assembled in different
fields, are not likely to have:

Caius (to his second, Jack Rugby): Vat is de clock, Jack?

Rugby: 'Tis past the hour, sir, that Sir Hugh promised to meet.

Caius: By gar, he has save his soul, dat he is no come; he has pray his
Pible well, dat he is no come: by gar, Jack Rugby, he is dead
already, if he be come.

Rugby: He is wise, sir; he knew your worship would kill him if he
came.

Caius: By gar, de herring is no dead so as I vill kill him.

to keep one's eyes skinned (or peeled)

To be very observant or extremely alert; to keep a sharp lookout. No record of this American expression has been turned up

earlier than 1833, but the fact that it then
appeared in a newspaper (*The Political
Examiner*, of Shelbyville, Kentucky) is a
fair indication that it was already well
known to any reader. The meaning was
not explained. The passage read: "I wish
I may be shot if I don't think you had
better keep your eyes skinned so that you
can look powerful sharp, lest we get rowed
up the river this heat."

deaf as an adder

"The wicked . . . go astray as soon as they be born, speaking
lies. Their poison is like the poison of a serpent: they are like the
deaf adder that stoppeth her ear; Which will not hearken to the
voice of the charmer, charming never so wisely." Psalms, lviii,
3–5. Or, in the language of the *Early English Psalter* (about 1300),

"Als of a neddre als-swa yat [that] stoppand es his eres twa." The allusion is to the ancient Oriental belief that certain serpents were able to protect themselves against being lured by the music of charmers by stopping up one ear with the tip of the tail and pressing the other firmly to the ground.

to go to the dickens

This is nothing more than a polite—or if not polite, at least euphemistic—way of saying "go to hell," or to perdition, or to the devil, or to ruin in some uncomfortable manner. It has nothing to do with the novelist, Charles Dickens, for "dickens," in this sense, was known to Shakespeare. He used it in *Merry Wives of Windsor,* Act III, scene 2, where Mrs. Page, in answer to Ford's, "Where had you this pretty weathercock," referring to Sir John Falstaff's page, Robin, replies, "I cannot tell what the dickens his name is my husband had him of."

But when and how "devil," or whatever the original term may have been, became distorted to "dickens" has not yet been determined. One conjecture is that the original term may have been "devilkins," little devil, which by frequent usage may have worn down to "dickens." We have many words in our present language derived through such a process, so this one sounds plausible—but, alas, no such use of "devilkins" or "deilkins" has turned up.

every dog has his day

The time will come to each of us to chuck one's weight around; to exhibit a period of ostentation, influence, or power. It may be long in the coming, but, according to this old proverb, everyone will at some time, at least once, be able to emulate the dog that, servile and cowed all its life, one day turns and snaps at its tormentor, or, perchance, struts proudly at the head of a ragamuffin procession. No one knows how old the proverb may be, nor, if not of English origin, from whence it came. It is found in *A Dialogue Conteynying Prouerbes and Epigrammes* (1562) by John Heywood —"But as euery man saith, a dog hath a daie"—and was used by Shakespeare: "The Cat will Mew, and Dogge will haue his day," in the words of Hamlet.

anvil chorus

The collective critical comments of those opposing any measure, political or otherwise; as, "Any proposal made by Franklin Roosevelt met with a resounding anvil chorus of Republican senators." The term has a musical background, referring originally to the cacophony of anvils or cymbals and timpani beaten rhythmically in the accompaniment of the so-called "Anvil Chorus," based on the "Gipsy Song" in Verdi's *Il Trovatore*. This familiar chorus runs:

> Proudly our banner now gleams with golden luster!
> Brighter each star shines in the glorious cluster!
> Hail, liberty forevermore!
> And Peace and Union
> And Peace and Union
> Throughout our happy land.

to bite off more than one can chew

To attempt more than one can accomplish; to try to do more than one has time for, or the ability for. A very human failing; one that is often quite praiseworthy, but also one that is often quite exasperating. The former could be said of a student, for  example, who, in the laudable desire to learn all he can, takes on more courses than he can find time to keep up with, and thus flunks several; the latter could be said of my more-than-willing yardman, Lou, who cannot say no to anyone seeking his services and, accordingingly, never turns up at an appointed date. The homely American expression has been traced back some seventy-five years, but is undoubtedly much earlier. It could have had a literal beginning with a small boy who took such a big mouthful as to be unable to do more than roll it around in his mouth; but more likely it started with a greedy person, say a Scotsman, who, borrowing a plug of tobacco, bit off too big a chunk to enjoy. (P.S. Lou isn't with me any more.)

pork barrel

According to the *Dictionary of American Politics* there was a time, on Southern plantations, back before the Civil War, when "the opening of a barrel of pork caused a rush to be made by the slaves." Mebbe so, though I doubt it. At any rate, even if so it had nothing to do with the present-day political implications of our phrase. Pork is fat, and "fat," for hundreds of years, has meant plenty, abundance—"Ye shall eat the fat of the land." Thus, anything especially lucrative or richly rewarding became "fat," and—a hundred years ago, especially in the halls of Congress—by simple transference became "pork."

Primarily, however, political "pork" in the luxuriant aftermath of the Civil War was any favor, distinction, or governmental money allotted to a district on no other basis than patronage. Later, roughly fifty years ago, when Congressmen began to seek larger appropriations to impress their constituents, as for river or harbor improvements, public buildings, or the like, such an appropriation became a "pork barrel."

even steven

With no advantage to either; as, to swap knives "even steven." Sometimes written with a capital, "Steven," and sometimes appearing as "Stephen." We've had the phrase as colloquial American for at least a hundred years, in print since 1866, but that is about all one can say of it. It is quite likely that it is nothing more than one of the numerous rhythmical reiteratives in the language, such as dilly-dally, shilly-shally, hodgepodge, 'ods bods, hocus-pocus, ding dong, hell's bells, and so on.

lame duck

'Way back in Revolutionary times, perhaps earlier, there was a woodsman maxim, "Never waste powder on a dead duck." From that, "dead duck" became popular slang, still in use, for anything —person or article—that is no longer worth a straw, that is done up, played out. Some bright wit a hundred years ago, probably a political writer with that slang term in mind, saw a chance for an apt modification. By the law that then existed (revised by the Twentieth Amendment, February 6, 1933), members of Congress who might fail of re-election in November, nevertheless still held office until March 4th following. Such outgoing "ducks" were not yet "dead," merely "lamed"; they could still, if sufficiently numerous, pass or propose legislation embarrassing to an incoming administration.

ham actor

One who is pretty far down the scale in acting ability. Sylva Clapin, in *A New Dictionary of Americanisms* (1902), defines such an actor, or the variant *ham:* "In theatrical parlance, a tenth-rate actor or variety performer." Why such a  term was so applied was long a matter of speculation, but it is now generally accepted that *ham* was an abbreviated form of the earlier appellation, *hamfatter,* a term that was especially applied to an actor of low grade, such as a Negro minstrel, back around 1875 and later. The early name derived from the fact that, for economic reasons, these actors used ham fat, instead of cold cream, to remove the necessarily liberal applications of make-up. The term *ham* is now also applied to third- or fourth-rate pugilists, ball-players, and other poorly skilled athletes or entertainers, and, though with no contempt, to the large army of well-equipped amateur radio operators, probably because, in the early days of radio, these operators were fumbling novices.

I declare to Betsy!

An ejaculation expressing positive affirmation, surprise, close interest, or similar emotion; equivalent to "Well, I do declare," etc. I am afraid that this Betsy, as also she of "Heavens to Betsy," was a homeless waif of no particular parentage. Like Topsy, she just "growed." "I declare to goodness," the bald "I declare," and the slightly stronger "Well, I declare" date back perhaps two or more centuries in the usage of England. "Declaring to goodness" savored too strongly of sacrilege to God-fearing American ears, but the innocuous Betsy was at hand, ready and willing.

three cheers and a tiger

The three cheers are self-explanatory, but why the "tiger"? It is, to be sure, a vociferous yell or howl added with utmost enthusiasm at the close of the cheering, perhaps emulating the roar or yowl of a genuine tiger. Well, here's the story, retold from Bartlett's *Dictionary of Americanisms* (1859):

The Boston Light Infantry visited Salem, Massachusetts, in 1822 and encamped in Washington Square. While there the soldiers indulged in some rough-and-tumble sports, probably playing to the gallery, and one of the young lady spectators called out, "Oh, you tiger!" to one of the most brawny of the young men. On the way back to Boston, some of the vocalists struck up an impromptu song, "Oh, you tigers, don't you know," to the tune of "Rob Roy McGregor, O!"—and the name stuck. In 1826 the Infantry visited New York where, at a public festival, the men concluded some maneuvers with the howl, the tiger's growl, that they had been rehearsing for four years. Thereafter, " 'three cheers and a tiger' are the inseparable demonstrations of approbation in that city [New York]."

on the cuff

On credit. I surmise, but can't prove, that this phrase and its interpretation originated in the barroom, the saloon of old. The bartender, short of convenient paper for keeping records of amounts due, but having starched white cuff and pencil handy, just wrote "John Jones—30" on his cuff, transferring the record to something more permanent when business was slack. *The American Thesaurus of Slang* (1947) says that the phrase also means "arranged; scheduled." I have never heard it so used.

to go hog wild

To become highly enthusiastic; especially, to become wildly excited, as hogs become when aroused; to run around like a chicken with its head cut off; hence, to become very angry, to get all het up;  also, to become profligate, to spend money like a drunken sailor. Both of my parents were born and reared in agricultural communities, and I am almost certain that this Americanism was familiar to each of them in all its senses. If so, that would take it back to the 1850's or 1860's. I am sure, however, that it was a familiar colloquialism to them in my early childhood, as I have known and used it all my life in each of its varied meanings. Nevertheless, the earliest printed date takes it back only to 1904, to a definition that appeared in *Dialect Notes,* with the single example: "I never saw such an excitement over a little thing in Arkansas as there was over that debate. They went hog wild." Perhaps some reader can cite an instance of earlier usage in print.

a stiff upper lip

Courage, or stoicism, which one keeps or carries. The significance of the idiom is well indicated by one of its earliest appearances in print—John Neal's *down Easters* (1833): "What's the use of boohooin'? . . . Keep a stiff upper lip; no bones broke—don't I know?"

"The die is cast!"

According to Plutarch's *Life of Julius Caesar,* this was the remark made by Caesar when, in 49 B.C., he decided to march toward Rome to protect himself against the machinations of Pompey. His words, of course, were in Latin—*"Alea est jacta!"*

Pompey, also a great Roman general, sharing with Caesar the control of the territories of Rome, wished to become sole dictator. To do so, he conspired first to destroy Caesar, then encamped for the winter, 50–49 B.C., with a portion of his army, beyond the northern boundary of Italy. Through faithful friends, Caesar learned of the conspiracy, made his fateful decision, and in January "crossed the Rubicon," the small river bordering Italy on the northeast. As he marched southward, city after city opened its gates in warm greeting, and Rome itself, with Pompey in flight, soon declared him sole dictator.

in the doldrums (or dumps)

Nowadays we say in the dumps, blue, low-spirited. Nobody knows what a *doldrum* was originally, but possibly the word itself was derived from *dull,* "stupid," or from the Middle English word *dold,* which had the same meaning. At any rate *doldrum* referred originally to a dull or sluggish person, a dullard. Literary use of the expression has been traced to less than a hundred and fifty years only, but I have a hunch that colloquial use goes back much further. We speak of a ship being "in the doldrums" when it is becalmed. This nautical usage, however, is of later vintage.

praise from Sir Hubert

The epitome of commendation; approval to the nth degree. The original Sir Hubert was a character in the eighteenth-century play, *A Cure for the Heartache,* written by Thomas Morton and first produced in London in 1797. Sir Hubert Stanley, in the play, was a kindly gentleman, filled with such gentility and beneficence that he was contantly in financial straits. However, he was noted for his sense of fairness to others regardless of his own circumstances, always prompt in rewarding merit, even though, as was often the case, it was verbal only. Our expression, slightly modified through the years, comes from the last scene of the last act. Sir Hubert says to Young Rapid, son of the tailor: "Mr. Rapid, by asserting your character as a man of honor, in rewarding the affection of this amiable woman, you command my praise; for bestowing happiness on my dear Charles, receive an old man's blessing." Young Rapid replies, "Approbation from Sir Hubert Stanley is praise indeed."

to have up one's sleeve

To have (something) in reserve in case of need; an alternative. Usually it is some bit of testimony, evidence, argument, plan, or project, or the like, that one has up his sleeve in readiness to spring or act upon if or when the original proposal turns out unsuccess-

fully. Or, in a bad sense, it may be that the villain in the play may have a scheme up his sleeve ready to spring and cause one's undoing. The allusion traces back to the costumes of the fifteenth century. In those days a man's garments were not made with the numerous pockets that modern man considers indispensable; in fact, there were none. Though some essential items were commonly hung from a belt, it was a god-send when some genius found that by making his often detachable sleeves slight-ly fuller between elbow and wrist he could tuck various necessities into those new-found pockets. The fashion went to ridiculous extremes, of course, with capacious sleeves sometimes almost scraping the ground. But while it lasted, until new styles came in with Henry VIII, man could conceal any variety of things up his sleeve.

to box the compass

To make a complete turn; also, to adopt successively all possible opinions on a question. Of course, any mariner would say that is all stuff and nonsense, and in his way of thinking he would be right. With him the phrase has just one meaning; to recite in order the thirty-two points of the compass, starting from north around through east, south, west, and back to north. But, of course, in doing so one describes a complete turn. The figurative sense has been with us since at least the beginning of the nineteenth century.

let sleeping dogs lie

To let a matter or person which at the present is at rest stay at rest, rather than to create a disturbance by bringing the matter up again or arousing the person. Chaucer wrote this in just the reverse form—"It is nought good a slepyng hound to wake" (*Troylus and Criseyde,* 1374)—and it was still so recorded some two hundred years later by John Heywood (*A Dialogue Conteynyng Prouerbes and Epigrammes,* 1562), "It is ill wakyng of a sleapyng dogge." But by the time of Charles Dickens (*David Copperfield,* 1850) it had been turned about into the order of today's usage.

no ifs, ans, nor buts

No back talk; no impudence; no argument. Our British cousins, from all that I can gather, limit this expression merely to "ifs and ans," as in the meaningless doggerel that my brother and I used to recite,

> If ifs and ans
> Were pots and pans,
> There'd be no use for tinkers.

—a slight variant, I believe, of an overseas doggerel. The older expression just means "if"; hence, a supposition. But our American expression is a negation and of much stronger force. A parent who uses it does so to end all argument: there'll be no *if* (no supposition), no *an* (an archaic form of *and,* hence, no condition), and no *but* (no exception).

love me, love my dog

Whatever my faults, if you love me you must put up with them. Regrettably, sometimes one's dearest friend or son or daughter construes this saying literally and thinks himself or herself quite at liberty, because of that friendship, to bring the hugest and smelliest Saint Bernard or flea-bitten pooch, shedding hair on rug or couch, into one's living-room. Perhaps some maiden fair did say it in a literal way to her gallant in the days when knighthood was in flower, but it is certainly not so meant nowadays. It is very old. Apperson found it in the writings (Latin) of Saint Bernard of Clairvaux (twelfth century): *Qui me amat, amat et canem meum,* and it occurs in the works of various English writers of the fifteenth and sixteenth centuries.

to carry the ball

To be responsible; to be in charge. The allusion is to the American game of football, to the player to whom, on a given play, the ball is assigned. Transference from literal to figurative usage became, at first, commercial lingo probably around 1925.

to tilt at windmills

To wage battle with chimeras; to take up the cudgels against an imaginary wrong or evil. The saying and its meaning take us to the redoubtable knight, Don Quixote, in the book of that name by Cervantes in 1605. The eighth chapter, Vol. I, begins: "At this point

they came in sight of thirty or forty windmills . . . and as soon as Don Quixote saw them he said to his squire, 'Fortune is arranging matters for us better than we could have shaped our desires ourselves, for look there, friend Sancho Panza, where thirty or more monstrous giants present themselves, all of whom I mean to engage in battle and slay, and with whose spoils we shall begin to make our fortunes; for this is righteous warfare, and it is God's good service to sweep so evil a breed off the face of the earth.' " Whereupon, despite the protestations of his squire, the resolute knight couched his lance, urged forward his good steed, Rosinante, and hurled himself at the arms of the nearest windmill. Clinging to the lance, he was lifted by the sail, until he dropped with a shattering thud to the earth—and had nothing but his pains for the effort.

double entendre

Those who use this term may find themselves scorned or held in ridicule by one who is really familiar with French. He will scoffingly say, "There is no such French expression. What you mean is 'double entente.' " The latter is, in fact, present French usage, but, nevertheless, back in the seventeenth century, as recorded by Littré, the French did say *"double entendre,"* and that was the term used in England by John Dryden during the same period and by later and present English and American writers. Our dictionaries give it some such definition as, "Double meaning; a statement or phrase so worded as to be capable of either of two interpretations, one quite innocent and the other, usually, of doubtful propriety."

hanged, drawn, and quartered

To be subjected to the direst penalty; originally a judgment rendered upon a criminal sentenced to death, but now often jocularly threatened to a person in mild reproof. The original sentence was anything but a joke. Prior to the fifteenth century it meant that the person so sentenced for a major crime was to be drawn at a horse's tail or upon a cart to the scene of execution, there to be hanged by the neck until dead, and his body then to be cut into four quarters and scattered into various parts of England. In later times a further penalty was allotted; the victim was first briefly hanged, then, while still living, he was disemboweled (*drawn*), then beheaded and quartered.

playing with loaded dice

Having little chance; playing a game of chance or engaging in any undertaking in which the odds are rigged against one. Obviously the expression derives from a game of dice in which the player who is discriminated against is given dice cleverly weighted which give him little or no chance to win. Thus *The Saturday Evening Post,* in an editorial, "Should America Remain in a Red-Operated UN?" (August 7, 1954), has the lines ". . . even if this were a game, who would go on playing after learning that the dice were loaded?"

time is of the essence

No doubt those who are accustomed to think of "essence" as being connected only with extracts of one kind or another, as essence of turpentine, essence of roses, find themselves at a loss when encountering this expression. But some eighty years ago—especially in the phrase "of the essence"—it was a legal term, and its meaning was virtually that of "essential." Hence, when you sign a contract containing the term, "time is of the essence," it would be well to understand that time is of the utmost importance in the fulfilment of that contract.

to set (persons) together by the ears

To involve them in a quarrel; set them at variance; create ill-will among them. The original ears were those of quarrelsome animals, those of cats especially, which tore at each other's ears when fighting. Thus Laurence Tomson in his translation (1579) of *Calvin's Sermons on the Epistles to Timothie and Titus* wrote, "When we be together by the eares like dogs and cattes."

to lift (or hoist or pull up) oneself by the bootstraps

You may travel all over the United States, North, South, East, or West, or in any part of Canada or England, and find almost no one who isn't familiar with one form or another of this expression. It is hardly necessary to say that by its use we mean to raise oneself  through one's unaided efforts above one's former cultural, social, or economic level. And yet, beyond being able to state positively that the expression cannot be more than three hundred and fifty years old, I cannot say in what English-speaking country it originated, or even whether it dates back to the time of George Washington and George the Third of England, though I am almost certain that it is considerably older. That is, I myself have not been able to turn up any printed use or record of this common expression at any date earlier than about ten years ago. It occurs on page 456 of *The Beards' Basic History of the United States* (1944) by Charles A. and Mary R. Beard. Undoubtedly it has appeared earlier, but no dictionary nor other reference work has made note of it. Yet I have seen it in print several times since that date.

In fact, I cannot even tell you nor hazard a guess as to how old the compound word *bootstrap* may be. The earliest printed record, so far as I have been able to discover, is in the *Funk & Wagnalls Standard Dictionary,* 1894 edition; and there it appears only in the definitions of two related words—*boot-hook* and *strap.* The first definition of *bootstrap* to appear in any dictionary is in the 1934 *Webster's New International Dictionary, Second Edition,* covering the familiar loop at the top of a boot.

But this strap was known to Shakespeare. In *Twelfth Night,* (1601), Act I, scene 3, Sir Toby Belch makes the comment: "These cloathes are good enough to drink in: and so bee these boots too; and they be not, let them hang themselues in their owne straps."

In an attempt to learn when such straps appeared on boots, I was referred eventually to Mr. John H. Thornton, M.A., F.B.S.I., Head of the Department of Boot and Shoe Manufacture, Northampton College of Technology, Northampton, England—a town where footwear has been made continuously since the thirteenth century and now the center of such manufacture in England. In the course of our correspondence Mr. Thornton wrote: "In my collection of boots and shoes I have a pair of Cromwellian riding boots *c.* 1653 and these have the loops (or the remnants of them) inside, so it is quite evident that boot-straps are as old as heavy riding boots themselves, which, as far as I can judge, came into use towards the end of the 16th century." Mr. Thornton also sent me photographs of one of those boots, side view and top view, from which the accompanying drawing was made.

Although, as another English correspondent seemed certain, this exploit of lifting oneself by one's own bootstraps is in line with other extravagant achievements of the eighteenth-century hero, Baron Munchausen, this feat is not to be found among the list. Did the expression not exist in 1785 when the book was written? or, as I think more likely, did the author, Rudolph Erich Raspe, not happen to think of it?

If an explanation is warranted, the expression alludes to the struggle from early date to late date in inserting one's foot into a well-fitting boot. The space at the right-angle turn from shank to sole is just not quite large enough for one's heel and ankle to slide through. The bootstrap was devised to give the would-be wearer a better purchase. Then came the boot-hook as illustrated, another early invention. But even with those aids he striving to wear the boot is sometimes uncertain whether he is trying to shove his foot downward or lift himself upward.

to hang on by the eyelashes

To be just barely able to retain one's hold on something, literal or figurative; to be in a precarious condition. Our ancestors, back in the seventeenth century "hung (something) by the eyelid," rather than the eyelashes, indicating that they meant to keep that thing or subject in suspense. Later, about a hundred years, "to hang by the eyelids" came into vogue with the meaning of our present expression. One fighting to retain a spark of life, or one barely able to stave off financial disaster is, with equal impartiality, "hanging on by his eyelashes."

to have many (or too many) irons in the fire

To undertake many things or have many activities under way at one time; also, to have alternate plans for gaining one's purpose; or, if we say "too many" rather than "many," to be engaged in more activities than one can properly manage; to bite off more than  one can chew. The allusion in any case is to the blacksmith. He who has many irons in his forge wastes little time. His well-trained apprentice maintains such control of the bellows and the placement of the irons that each is ready in turn at the anvil and hammer. Or if, perchance, an armorer were engaged in forging a suit of armor, he would be ready, if skilled, to take whatever piece of steel came from the forge and shape it to best advantage, whether for greave, cuirass, vambrace, or gauntlet. "Too many irons in the fire" would mark an inefficient smith or one with an unskilled apprentice. Figurative use of either saying takes us back only to the middle of the sixteenth century.

to paint the lily

Yes, that's the way Shakespeare wrote it; not as one so often hears it, "to gild the lily." It's to be found in *King John,* Act IV, scene 2. The king who seized the throne unjustly after the death of his brother Richard in 1199 believed toward the close of his reign that a second coronation might strengthen his position and bolster the waning affections of his subjects. Lords Pembroke and Salisbury, among others, thought that to be an altogether superfluous gesture, and Salisbury added:

> Therefore, to be possess'd with double pomp,
> To guard a title that was rich before,
> To gild refined gold, to paint the lily,
> To throw a perfume on the violet,
> To smooth the ice, or add another hue
> Unto the rainbow, or with taper-light
> To seek the beauteous eye of heaven to garnish,
> Is wasteful, and ridiculous excess.

full of prunes (or beans)

Each has the same meaning—peppy, lively, energetic, in high spirits, feeling one's oats, rarin' to go. "Beans" was the first, and was originally said of horses after a feeding of beans raised for fodder—"horse beans," so called. Undoubtedly the spirited state of a bean-fed horse was observed in remote times—Romans also used beans as fodder—but I find nothing equivalent to the current expression before its own rise less than a hundred years ago. ("Full of beans" is now also used slangily to mean foolish or silly, possibly because a person in high spirits often permits his superabundant energy to express itself ridiculously.) The substitution of "prunes" came into use at least seventy years ago, but a satisfactory reason for it is difficult to determine. Perhaps the dietary effect of an overindulgence in this comestible may have had something to do with it. I am reminded, at least, of a mother who urged her son, training for scholastic track events: "Eat plenty of prunes, Jimmy; they'll make you run."

Lucullian feast (or banquet)

A feast of inordinate magnificence; a terrific spread. L. Licinus Lucullus was a great Roman general in the early part of the first century B.C., and was at first famous for his victories over Mithridates. His victories brought him great wealth, and after his retirement he embarked upon an unprecedented scale of living and sensual indulgence. "A single supper in the hall," according to Smith's *Dictionary of Greek and Roman Mythology and Biography,* "was said to cost the sum of 50,000 denarii." Such prodigality, especially when frequently repeated, was notable even in a period marked by magnificence. Thus, though his military prowess is almost forgotten, his name still lives in the language through his reputation as a glutton.

to take forty winks

Though I'm not saying that the reading of the Thirty-nine Articles has an actual bearing on the "forty winks" or short nap that is likely to succeed that reading—or interrupt it—such a sequel could be inferred. The Thirty-nine Articles, for the benefit of the unenlightened, are the articles of faith of the Church of England which the clergy are required to accept. Adoption became legal by parliamentary action in 1571 in the reign of Elizabeth I. Needless to say, the perusal of these articles is likely to be considered most dreary. At least they led a writer in *Punch* (November 16, 1872) to say: "If a . . . man, after reading through the Thirty-nine Articles, were to take forty winks"—and that is the first literary record of this precise number of winks.

fit (or fine) as a fiddle

In fine form or condition; in splendid health. Although "fiddles" were known in England back at least in the early thirteenth century, it was some four hundred years later, evidently, before their shape, form, tone, and other qualities became so pleasing as to invite complimentary applications to humans. "To have one's face made of a fiddle" was to be exceptionally good looking. "To play first fiddle" was to occupy a leading position, and one "fit as a fiddle" or "fine as a fiddle" was beyond further need of improvement in health or condition. Apperson traces the metaphor to Haughton's *England for My Money* (1616), "This is excellent, i' faith; as fit as a fiddle."

not to care a fiddlestick

To be wholly unconcerned; to care nothing at all. Although our ancestors, some three hundred years ago, had high regard for the fiddle, they seemed to think of the fiddlestick, without which the fiddle could not be played, as a mere trifle, a bagatelle, something so insignificant as to be absurd. Thus, Grose, in his *Classical Dictionary of the Vulgar Tongue* (1796) defined *fiddlestick's end* as "Nothing." Washington Irving, in *Salmagundi* (1806–1807) is credited with the introduction of the present phrase into the literary language.

on the fritz

Out of order; gone haywire; on the kibosh; not in good health or in good condition. According to my best recollections and those of others whom I have consulted, this expression entered the American language about the turn of the century, though it seems to have escaped the notice of recorders of the language. Who the "Fritz" was whose fame thus became immortalized is now, alas, lost to memory dear. To be sure Fritz of the Katzenjammer twins had even then begun to grace the pages of the New York *Journal,* but, though guilty along with Hans of every mischief in the calendar, he was ever in abounding health—definitely not the source of this commemoration.

56 ·

a shot in the arm

Somewhere I read that this was derived from the hypodermic injection of a drug administered by a physician for the prevention or cure of a disease or the alleviation of pain. To be sure, the

expression is used with such meaning, but I don't think that the original "shot" was with such purpose. It was administered by a hypodermic syringe, all right, but with a "Quick, Watson, the needle!" intent— the injection of any drug that would induce exhilaration. In my opinion, that is, the expression, which is not more than about forty years old, was derived from drug addiction, though it is applied now, not only to medical injections as for vaccination, etc., but also to the taking of any stimulant, such as coffee, a "Coke," or an intoxicant—in the latter instance replacing the older "shot in the neck."

rag-tag and bobtail

First, away back in the sixteenth century, it was "tag and rag," or sometimes just "tag," always meaning the rabble, the common herd, the riffraff of society, the people generally held in low esteem. Thus we read: "To walles they go, both tagge and ragge, their Citie to defende" and "Huntyd, and killyd tage and rage with honds and swords." And this remained the usual order for the next two hundred years. In the time of the diarist, Samuel Pepys, however, the expression was further intensified by "bobtail," a term that had originally applied to the tail of a horse, cut short, and later used alone as a synonym for "tag and rag." Thus Pepys wrote (1660), "The dining room . . . was full of tag, rag, and bobtail, dancing, singing, and drinking." Early in the nineteenth century, probably for greater euphony, the first two terms became reversed, usually written as in the heading here, though from a grammatical view we should write "rag, tag, and bobtail."

the fat is in the fire

The mischief is done and unpleasant results must be faced; an irretrievable blunder has been made and ill consequences will follow; some dire act has been committed which will undoubtedly provoke an explosion of anger. No one knows how old this saying may be, and the beginning can only be guessed. It was recorded in John Heywood's *A Dialogue Conteynyng Prouerbes and Epigrammes* (1562), and, accordingly, must have long been in use before that time. But in those days the saw meant that some project had failed and one must cut his cloth accordingly. Heywood wrote, "Than [Then] farewell riches, the fat is in the fire." One may surmise, probably correctly, that the original allusion was to a chunk of fat meat which, thrust through by a spit on the hearth to roast, caught ablaze and fell into the fire to the dismay of the cook.

root hog or die

Get to work or suffer the consequences. Although the earliest printed record of the Americanism so far exhumed dates only to 1834—"We therefore determined to go on the old saying, root hog or die": *A Narrative of the Life of David Crockett*—it probably goes back to colonial times or, at least, to early frontier days. And, probably, its origin was literal—an admonition to hogs or pigs when crops were scant to forage for themselves in order to survive. In fact, the expression sometimes appears as a command as given to a hog: "Root, hog, or die!" The way it appears in each of the seven stanzas of the folk song under that title in the Archive of the American Folk Song Society, Library of Congress, each of which closes with the line, is:

> Oh, I went to Californy in the spring of Seventy-six,
> Oh, when I landed there I wuz in a terrible fix.
> I didn't have no money my victuals for to buy,
> And the only thing for me was to root, hog, or die.

to cut (or split) a melon

This is a delightful procedure, both for the cutter and for him who receives a portion of the melon. He, or more likely they, in charge of the cutting is delighted that there is something to cut, and the receiver always has had a mouth watering for the taste. In other words, this was originally Wall Street jargon meaning to distribute dividends—especially extra dividends—to the stockholders of an enterprise. As such, the term came into use about 1906. Nowadays we also use it to mean to distribute profits of any kind to any entitled to receive them—usually the heads or principal officers of an organization, the employees, the financial backers, etc.

skeleton in the closet

What started this expression, no one knows. Perhaps it was an actual incident; perhaps a real skeleton was found walled up in the closet of some country house concealing some long-hidden family shame or sorrow. At any rate, *The Oxford English Dictionary* says

that this expression and its meaning are known to have been in use before 1845, though it was in that year that the earliest printed usage was recorded. That was by William Makepeace Thackeray in one of his contributions to the magazine, *Punch*. But the expression undoubtedly struck his fancy, as he used it again as the heading of Chapter LV, "Barnes's Skeleton Closet," in *The Newcomes* (1855). However, the "skeleton" in Sir Barnes Newcome's closet would not receive much consideration in any but a highly sensitive family. It was merely that he, though "the reigning prince" of the Newcome family after his father's death, was not well received by the townfolk and country gentry of Newcome, because of his own arrogance, along with a bullying attitude toward his wife. The chapter relates, in the author's words, "Some particulars regarding the Newcome family, which will show that they have a skeleton or two in *their* closets, as well as their neighbours."

Johnny-come-lately

A newcomer; one recently arrived; an inexperienced person. Apparently this was originally, in the early quarter of the nineteenth century, the American sailor's version of the British "Johnny Newcome," any recruit aboard any of His Majesty's vessels. Our earliest instance of usage appears in *The Adventures of Harry Franco* (1839), by the journalist, Charles F. Briggs: " 'But it's Johnny Comelately, aint it, you?' said a young mizzen topman."

to dance Juba

Just as Cuffee (or Cuffy), back in the days of slavery, was the name often given by Negroes to a boy born on Friday, so Juba was the name of African origin frequently given to girls born on Monday (see Hennig Cohen in *American Speech,* XXVII, 103–04). But, unlike the white child born on Monday who, in the old folk rhyme, is "fair of face," the black girl child was, presumably, a natural-born imp of perversity and had, repeatedly, to be switched. Thus, "to dance Juba," which, in the early days of minstrel shows of the 1830's, meant to dance in a rollicking manner with hands, feet, and head all in motion, appears to have had its start in the animated dancing performed involuntarily by a child being switched in punishment for some kind of naughtiness of deviltry. Such, at least, is the interpretation of Dr. Mitford M. Mathews (in *American Speech* XXVIII, 206), speaking from personal experience of his boyhood in Alabama about 1900.

like greased lightning

Lickety-split; like a blue streak; like a bat out of hell; with extreme rapidity. Although this has the appearance of typical American exaggerated hyperbole, nevertheless the earliest printed record of use is in the *Boston, Lincoln, and Louth Herald,* published in Lincolnshire, England, the issue of January 15, 1833: "He spoke as quick as greased lightning." We must have taken it to our own bosoms shortly after its coinage, however, for it flourisheth here like the green bay tree.

Main Liner

If you are one of these, in or around Philadelphia, then you really belong. You are a member of the Upper Crust, one who can look down your nose at any other class of persons in Pennsylvania, at least, and perhaps elsewhere—except, possibly, a person from Boston's Back Bay or an F.F.V. (First Family of Virginia). That is to say, by way of explanation, you live along the "main line" of the Pennsylvania Railroad, in the beautiful suburban area just outside Philadelphia. The cognomen for these highly aristocratic, ultra-conservative members of society has been in use since early in this century—but the distinction is fading, as elsewhere.

to kick against the pricks

To use vain efforts; be recalcitrant; knock one's head against a wall; suffer from one's own misdeeds; kick against thorns or spurs to one's own hurt. Saul, later called Paul, on his way to Damascus from Jerusalem, where he had received letters authorizing him to arrest any Christians and take them to Jerusalem for trial, was stopped on the road by a messenger from God, as related in Acts ix, "and suddenly there shined round him a light from heaven: And he fell to the earth, and heard a voice saying unto him, Saul, Saul, why persecuteth thou me? And he said, Who art thou, Lord? And the Lord said, I am Jesus whom thou persecuteth: it is hard for thee to kick against the pricks."

to turn a new leaf

To amend one's conduct; begin a new life; go straight; reform. The leaf that one turns is not that of a tree, but that of a book, a book of lessons or of precepts, the book on which our sins of omission and commission are recorded. And we have been doing that, or at least using that expression for something over four hundred years. Though not the earliest example, we find the expression in Raphael Holinshed's *Chronicles of England, Scotlande, and Irelande* (1577), "He must turne the leafe, and take out a new lesson, by changing his former trade of liuing into better."

to gird (up) one's loins

Another Biblical phrase that has been taken in its early figurative sense directly into the language. He who "girds up his loins" prepares for action, usually physical and strenuous, but it may also be mental. In the physical sense the allusion was to the workman who, in preparation for work, tucked the long skirt of his garment into his girdle or belt. The reference is to Proverbs xxxi, 17, which in the Coverdale translation (1535) reads: "She gyrdeth hir loynes with strength."

on the carpet

In the days when "carpet" retained its original sense, "a thick fabric used to cover tables," to have something "on the carpet" had the same meaning that we now give to "on the table"; that is, to have something up for discussion, for consideration. Such was the  usage in the early eighteenth century and is still common usage in England, and is, as well, the intent of the French *sur le tapis,* and the German *aufs Tapet.* But dainty ladies found, even in the fifteenth century, that these thick fabrics also made ideal floor coverings and began to use them, first, in their bedchambers, and then in other private or formal rooms of a house. But they were for the use of the gentry. The occasions when a servant might "walk the carpet," as the expression went, was when he or she was called before the mistress or master of the house for a reprimand. Though this latter expression, coined in the early nineteenth century, is still in use, it has been largely replaced, especially in America, by transferring its meaning to "on the carpet."

on the level (on the square)

In all sincerity, honesty, or truth; on the up-and-up; the real McCoy. Both of these expressions were taken from the ritual of Freemasonry and both are of legendary antiquity. In the rites of the lodges, however, the level, an instrument used by builders to determine a common plane, is actually a symbol of equality. The square, an instrument of equally great precision for determining accurately an angle of ninety degrees, the fourth part of a circle, is a symbol of morality, truth, and honesty. *The Encyclopedia of*

Freemasonry (1916 edition) relates: "In the year 1830, the architect, in rebuilding a very ancient bridge called Baal Bridge, near Limerick, in Ireland, found under the foundation-stone an old brass square, much eaten away, containing on its two surfaces the following inscription [dated 1517]:

> I. WILL. STRIUE. TO. LIUE.—
> WITH. LOUE. & CARE.—
> UPON. THE. LEUL.—
> BY. THE. SQUARE.

a lick and a promise

This is the act that Johnny—or Billy, or Jeff, or Chip—generally does with a washcloth. Just a hasty dab—enough, he hopes, to pass grandma's not too critical eye before sliding into his place at the table. The "lick," that is, has nothing to do with a thrashing, but pertains rather to the rapid lapping of the tongue such as that of a cat drinking milk. It's a small quantity or small amount, about the amount we mean when we say that so-and-so hasn't "a lick of sense." The "promise," of course, is in Johnny's indefinite future, something that may be long deferred. And both "lick" and "promise" may apply to any chore. Nor is the action limited to young males. It may apply to a chore performed incompletely or inadequately by anyone. The expression dates back at least to 1850.

nip and tuck

Of course every American knows that this means neck and neck, or just about as close a finish in any sort of competition as two or more contestants could get—a photo finish, in modern terminology. But why "nip," and why "tuck"? There have been variations of the expression in the hundred and twenty-odd years of recorded usage. James K. Paulding in *Westward Ho!* (1832), gives it, "There we were at rip and tuck, up one tree and down another." William T. Porter, a dozen years or so later, wrote it both "nip and tack" and "nip and chuck." But "nip and tuck" has been common usage through the years since. The dictionaries, playing safe, refuse even to guess at the source, but I'll stick my neck out to suggest that perhaps Paulding was right. A rip, of course, is the result of what mother does to a piece of cloth in reducing it to smaller portions; the tuck the fold she makes in one such portion to sew it to another, as in making a patchwork quilt. By successive rips and tucks the patchwork comes out even. Pretty thin? Well, even some dictionary derivations with all steps known look superficially thinner.

to play fast and loose

"Fast and loose" was the name of an old cheating game, known in the middle of the sixteenth century at least. The game was thus explained by James O. Halliwell in his *Dictionary of Archaic and Provincial Words, Obsolete Phrases, Proverbs and Ancient Customs, from the Fourteenth Century* (1847): "A cheating game played with a stick and a belt or string, so arranged that a spectator would think he could make the latter fast by placing a stick through its intricate folds, whereas the operator could detach it at once." In fact, the game must have been known at a considerably earlier period, for the present phrase in a metaphorical sense—to say one thing and do another; to be slippery as an eel; to have loose morals —appeared in one of the epigrams in *Tottel's Miscellany* (1547): "Of a new married student that plaied fast or loose"—i.e., was unfaithful.

according to one's lights

When I was young, this always struck me as a silly expression. The "lights" were the last things—bright red and closely adhering —that my mother removed in cleaning a fowl, the "liver and lights" always in combination. It was not until some years later that I learned that "lights" is an old, a very old, term for "lungs." In fact, it dates back to the twelfth century. Our present phrase has nothing to do with that usage. Here it is the light of knowledge that is meant; one's opinions, information, abilities, capacities, or the like.

plain as the nose on one's face

Ridiculously obvious; as conspicuous or evident as anything could possibly be. The comparison must have been known to Shakespeare, who used it ironically in *Two Gentlemen of Verona* (1591). The Lady Sylvia had enjoined Valentine, who loves her, "to write some lines to one she loves." She affects to be displeased with the result, though Valentine's servant sees plainly that the one she loves is his master. When Sylvia leaves, the servant says:

> O jest unseen, inscrutable, invisible
> As a nose on a man's face, or a weathercock on a steeple!
> My master sues to her; and she hath taught her suitor,
> He being her pupil, to become her tutor.
> O excellent device! was there ever heard a better,
> That my master, being scribe, to himself should write the letter?

meddlesome Matty

One who sticks his (or, more likely, her) nose into the affairs of others; or, among the young, one who inordinately busies oneself with or constantly fingers objects belonging to others. The term  derived from a poem of that title, written by Ann Taylor, first appearing in *Original Poems for Infant Minds,* published in 1804–05, and written chiefly by members of the family of Isaac Taylor, English engraver. Among them, incidentally, was the well-known "Twinkle, twinkle, little star, How I wonder what you are," written by Ann's younger sister, Jane. The nine verses of "Meddlesome Matty," too extensive to be quoted here, are recommended reading for all, children or adults, who have been accused of possessing such propensities:

> Oh, how one ugly trick has ſpoil'd
> The ſweeteſt and the beſt!
> Matilda, tho' a pleaſant child,
> One ugly trick poſſeſſ'd,
> Which like a cloud before the ſkies,
> Hid all her better qualities.
>
> Sometimes ſhe'd lift the teapot lid,
> To peep at what was in it;
> Or tilt the kettle, if you did
> But turn your back a minute.

In vain you told her not to touch,
Her trick of meddling grew ſo much.

But Matilda went too far eventually and got her comeuppance:

Her grandmamma went out one day,
And by miſtake ſhe laid
Her ſpectacles and ſnuff-box gay
Too near the little maid . . .

She donned the "glaſſes," and "looking round, as I ſuppoſe, The ſnuff box too ſhe ſpied." Nothing would do, of course, but open it.

So thumb and finger went to work
To move the stubborn lid;
And preſently, a mighty jirk,
The mighty miſchief did:
For all at once, ah! woeful caſe,
The ſnuff came puffing in her face!
. . . .
In vain ſhe ran about for eaſe,
She could do nothing elſe but ſneeze!

no skin off one's nose

Nothing of concern to one; not one's affair. In today's slang, nose is sometimes replaced by ear, elbow, or back, but the implication is equally evident: If one doesn't butt into, or stick one's nose into, an affair that is none of one's business, he is not likely to suffer abrasions upon any prominent portion of his anatomy by being thrown out upon his nose, elbow, back, shoulder, or the like. The allusion is American, at least fifty years old.

lares and penates

The familiar things, the cherished possessions, the appearance, the indescribable atmosphere which combine to make a house a home. Actually, this phrase combines two groups of Roman gods, though minor gods, to be sure. The *lares* (two syllables, please— lar'eez) were divinities presiding over the hearth and the whole house, representing the spirits, not of all the ancestral dead lords of the house, but only of good men. The *penates* (three syllables—

pe-nah'teez) were the protectors and promoters of happiness, peace, and concord in the family.

Tell it to the Marines

A fish story: an expression of disbelief or incredulity. Lord Byron, in *The Island* (1823), who appears to have been the first to record the expression, added the note: " 'That will do for the marines, but the sailors won't believe it,' is an old saying." A year later, in *Redgauntlet,* Sir Walter Scott repeats it thus: "Tell that to the marines—the sailors won't believe it." The inference is most powerful that the British Royal Marines of that period were such gullible landlubbers that they would swallow any yarn hook, line, and sinker.

a fish out of water

One out of one's element or the setting or environment to which one is accustomed. But unlike the aquatic animal yanked from stream, pool, or sea, the person who merely feels like a fish out  of water rarely suffers death from the sensation, no matter how protracted. The metaphor in English is found as far back as the *English Works* of John Wyclif (*c.* 1380): "And how thei weren out of ther cloistre as fishis withouten water." But Apperson carries it back to the Greek patriarch, St. Athanasius, of the fourth century, though citing no reference, and thinks it may have had an even earlier Greek form. He connects it, amusingly, to the Latin expression, *mus in matella,* a mouse in the pot: said of a person who finds himself in a pretty predicament.

Mardi gras

Mardi, Tuesday, and *gras,* fat; hence, "fat Tuesday," as is the literal meaning in France—"Shrove Tuesday," as we call the day before the beginning of Lent in English. No one knows when these days of carnival began, though probably they are a survival of the Roman festival of Lupercal held at the same season of the year. The name is derived from an immemorial custom in Paris, now little observed, of leading an especially fattened ox (*boeuf gras*) at the head of the carnival procession of merrymakers. But except in certain cities of Italy and in New Orleans in the United States, where the carnival procession and merrymaking essay annually to outdo all predecessors, the customs of former years have gradually been dropped.

to throw a monkey wrench in the machinery

To gum up the works; to place an obstacle or hindrance into a project or undertaking; to interfere, or cause confusion or disaster. Undoubtedly this literally described an act of sabotage when it was first used—possibly no more than fifty years ago, though it seems to me I have known it all my life. However, I may be mistaken, as the earliest literary use so far dug up, and the figurative use at that, was only twenty-five years ago. Garry Allighan, in his *The Romance of the Talkies* (1929), wrote: "The Talkies threw several kinds of monkey wrenches into the machinery of production." The expression is undoubtedly American, as the British say "spanner wrench" for the same type of wrench.

Furthermore, though the source of the name of the implement is not certain, there is good reason to think it American, as well as the implement itself. The tool was known in 1858, and Dr. M. M. Mathews, writing in *American Speech* (February, 1953), refers to an item that appeared in the Boston *Transcript* sometime in the winter of 1932–33, which credits the invention to a man named Monk, in 1856, employed by Bemis & Call of Springfield, Massachusetts. The item adds that the wrench was first called *Monk's wrench,* later jocularly turned into *monkey wrench.* But Dr. Mathews makes it clear that he has no confirmation of this tale.

as mad as hops

Confoundedly irate; mad enough to bite nails; roaring mad. Although "as thick as hops" has a literal background, referring either to the density of the hedges or thickets of hop vines as grown in southern England especially, or to the close growth of the cones on the vines, and although "as fast as hops" pertains to the rapid growth of the hop vine, this present expression has no such relationship. Some distinguished individual, probably American— wholly unknown now, but with a sly bit of punning humor in his make-up—coined it some seventy or seventy-five years ago by giving a slight twist to the well-known "hopping mad," so mad, irate, or angry that one fairly dances or hops around, sputtering with rage. The first occurrence in print was in a story by an unnamed writer in the October, 1884, issue of *Harper's New Monthly Magazine*. It's a story about a youngster called Gus who is annoyed with a pupil who is teasing the teacher.

Agnes looked at her for a minute. Then she tried to speak, but she broke down, and laughed instead. The tears rolled down her cheeks, but she laughed on, for all she was sobbing at the same time. Then she just jumped up and ran out of the room. Lil she turned round and grinned at me—such a grin! It made me mad as hops.

to put one's foot in it

If your wife kicks you under the table or otherwise makes it plain to you that it would be best not to go on with what you were about to say, you may, she hopes, understand that she's trying to

head you off from "putting your foot in it," from committing a social blunder or doing something that had best be left unsaid or undone. The figurative phrase was in current use in the latter part of the eighteenth century, but what the original allusion was is anyone's guess. Personally, because such a blunder fits so patly, I have always been taken by an old rancher's literal description of a hand he had recently hired: "I declare, he's such an ass that if there was just one cow-flop in a ten-acre field he'd be sure to put his foot in it."

Mother Carey's chicken

Both this name bestowed by sailors, two hundred or more years ago, and the regular name, the storm petrel, carry us to the New Testament. *Petrel*, French for "little Peter," was so named from its seeming to walk on the water like the disciple Peter, as related in Matthew xiv, 29. And *Mother Carey* (or *Cary*) was the British seaman's version of the title often used by Levantine sailors, *Mater cara*, "beloved Mother." The small bird, so the sailors believed, exhibited great activity at the approach of a storm.

easy as rolling off a log

Nothing could be easier; the simplest action possible. Early American colonists, probably, moving into a wilderness with a hundred things to be done at once by both husband and wife, sought desperately for a safe and dry place to "park" the baby

temporarily. Just as a modern couple would do on a camping expedition, undoubtedly they would place the infant on a log—"just for a minute." The little round bottom of the baby, however, was no more stable on the big round log than a marble would be on a child's balloon. At least, this could have been the way the metaphor started, for it goes back into colonial days.

not for money, marbles, nor chalk

Not for any consideration whatever; absolutely not; utterly incorruptible. Although "marbles," in this expression, could be taken to mean "slight value," with "chalk" indicating "no value," I think it more likely to be a slight mispronunciation of *meubles*, a term of French origin used both in France and England to mean "personal property." Thus the expression would literally mean, "not for real property, personal property, nor useless property."

high jinks

Mad frolic; pranks; jollity. At the end of the seventeenth century this was a term applied at drinking bouts for the ludicrous performance put on by some members of the party selected for the purpose by a throw of dice. It is best described in *Guy Mannering* (1815) by Sir Walter Scott: "On the present occasion, the revel had lasted since four o'clock, and, at length, under the direction of a venerable compotator . . . the frolicsome company had begun to practise the ancient and now forgotten pastime of *High Jinks.* The game was played in several different ways. Most frequently the dice were thrown by the company, and those upon whom the lot fell were obliged to assume and maintain for a time a certain fictitious character, or to repeat a certain number of fescennine verses in a particular order. If they departed from the character assigned, or if their memory proved treacherous in the repetition, they incurred forfeits, which were compounded for by swallowing an additional bumper, or by paying a small sum toward the reckoning."

to get a kick (or charge) out of (something)

To become thrilled, excited, or stimulated by something physical, mental, or emotional. The older American slang with "kick" is gradually being replaced by the later "charge," having the same interpretation, but "kick" has served well for some fifty years. Originally the "kick" was that induced by spirituous liquor, or perhaps by a sharp condiment, and the effect was physical, though considerably milder than if delivered by a horse or mule or even a high-powered gun. Our metaphorical expression has also been accepted by English writers, as, for instance, by a correspondent to the *Daily Express* in 1928: "I was told I should get a kick out of that journey —and I certainly did."

to put one through a course of sprouts

To give one a thorough and disciplined course of training. In my earlier book, *A Hog on Ice,* I offered no explanation of the source of this phrase. Mary Gilbert Smith of Wallingford, Vermont, author of the series of Grandpa White stories which appeared for some years in the Boston *Globe,* states in a letter to me that it stems from the days when plowing and heavy farm work in New England were done with oxen. "If a yoke of oxen," she wrote, "proved obstrep-

erous, an easy cure was to drive them through a course of sprouts—
i.e., young trees springing up where the forest had been cut over.
My uncle told me a story of my great-uncle, John Quincy Adams,
who taught a yoke that wouldn't hold back on a hill by driving
them down so fast that they couldn't turn at the 'elbow,' as was
their amiable custom, but plunged into the maple sprouts below
the road—tough young sprouts that switched them thoroughly before they came to a stop. Thereafter no yoke was more docile."

No doubt "a course of sprouts" could refer to a row or line of
young trees or brush; nevertheless I do not see how oxen or other
animals could be lashed or switched by such a growth in dashing—
or lumbering—through it, as Mrs. Smith recites, though their over-
zealousness would certainly be tempered.

dead man (or soldier)

Just a liquor bottle—or, perhaps nowadays, can—that is empty;
hence, worthless, good for nothing, as a dead man or soldier on a
battlefield would be. The term was recognized in *A New Dictionary
of the Terms Ancient and Modern of the Canting Crew,* printed
about 1700, and must certainly have been used many years earlier
to have received a listing in that collection.

neat but not gaudy

A friend, just returned from a trip to Spain, said to me, "Know
what I saw in Barcelona, Charles? The mansion from which we got
the word *gaudy*! Put up by a grandee named Gaudi." I said, "Well,
it must be pretty old, then." "No," said he, "just recently finished."
He was quite taken aback to learn that the word had been in our
language at least four hundred years. But the present expression is
not that old. Probably Charles Lamb started it. In one of his letters,
written in 1806, he mentioned "A little thin flowery border round,
—neat, not gaudy."

Several years later, whether from Lamb's phrase or not, the more
popular expression, still in use in one form or another, came into
circulation. It first appeared in print in an article written for the
staid *Magazine of Architecture,* November 1838, by the nineteen-

year-old John Ruskin, later noted as an art critic. He wrote: "That admiration of the 'neat but not gaudy,' which is commonly reported to have influenced the devil when he painted his tail pea green."

My own usage, from first hearing some fifty years ago, has always been, "Neat but not gaudy, as the devil said when he painted his tail sky-blue." More decorous speakers substitute "monkey." And the tail may be painted in any color of the rainbow.

to pull a boner

To blunder; to make a stupid or ridiculous mistake; also, to be a bonehead. By deduction, I figure that this American phrase, of about fifty years' standing, came from "Bones" or "Mistah Bones"

of the old-style minstrel show. Originally there was but one of him, the end man in the show who played the "bones"—two pairs of ebony sticks (or, sometimes, pieces of seasoned and polished rib bones), about one inch wide and six inches long, clapped together in the performer's fingers. The other end man was "Tambo" or "Mistah Tambo," from the tambourine played by him. Both end men were later called "Bones," but in either case the "interlocutor," sitting in the middle of the line, directed such questions at the end men as would bring out jests or would evoke ridiculous answers or stupid blunders. He would, that is, "pull boners" from them.

to raise (or play) hob

To raise Cain; play the devil; make mischief. In English folklore, "Hob" was the familiar name of the sprite, Robin Goodfellow, the household spirit full of mischievous, sometimes malicious, acts—the being who, at least, received the blame. Shakespeare, in *A Midsummer Night's Dream,* gives him also his earliest English name, Puck, dating back at least to the eleventh century, and thus describes him in Act II, scene 1:

· 73

Fairy: Either I mistake your shape and making quite,
Or else you are that shrewd and knavish sprite
Call'd Robin Goodfellow: are not you he
That frights the maidens of the villagery;
Skim milk, and sometimes labour in the quern,
And bootless make the breathless housewife churn;
And sometime make the drink to bear no barm,
Mislead night-wanderers, laughing at their harm?
Those that Hobgoblin call you, and sweet Puck,
You do their work, and they shall have good luck:
Are not you he?

Puck: Thou speak'st aright;
I am that merry wanderer of the night.
I jest to Oberon, and make him smile,
When I a fat and bean-fed horse beguile,
Neighing in likeness of a silly foal:
And sometimes lurk I in a gossip's bowl,
In very likeness of a roasted crab;
And when she drinks, against her lips I bob
And on her withered dewlap pour the ale.
The wisest aunt, telling the saddest tale,
Sometime for three-foot stool mistaketh me;
Then slip I from her bum, down topples she,
And "tailor" cries, and falls into a cough;
And then the whole quire hold their hips and laugh;
And waxen in their mirth, and neeze, and swear
A merrier hour was never wasted there.

without rhyme or reason

Lacking in sense or justification. The French still say, *ni rime ni raison;* but we borrowed the saying from the French of the late Middle Ages, *na Ryme ne Raison,* as reported by W. W. Skeat some years ago in *Notes & Queries.* English usage dates from the early sixteenth century.

a hurrah's nest

A disorderly, untidy mess; a place of wild confusion. This "nest" has been variously attributed to a *hurrah,* a *hurra,* and a *hoorah,* but, I regret to say, no naturalist or folklorist has ever yet attempted to describe the imaginary creature responsible for the untidiness. My one-time associates, compilers of *The Standard Dictionary of Folklore* (1949–50), ignore it. In fact, because it first appeared in Samuel Longfellow's biography of his brother, Henry Wadsworth Longfellow, in 1829, and next in *Twenty Years Before the Mast* (1840), by Richard Henry Dana, who was a student at Harvard under H. W. Longfellow, it may well be that the "hurra's nest," as the biographer wrote it, was a family term that entered unconsciously into the ordinary conversation of members of the Longfellow family and was picked up by others who heard them use it. Our language does sometimes grow in that manner.

to quarrel with one's bread and butter

To complain about one's means of livelihood; to act against one's best interests. And many's the time you've seen a child do that— throw his buttered bread or his piece of cake or even the ice-cream cone he's been whimpering for on the ground in a fit of rage. The human race has been thus quarreling since the days of Noah, but our English phrase for expressing such lack of reason dates back not more than two centuries.

to the queen's taste

To a fare-you-well; lock, stock, and barrel; completely; utterly; totally. There was no individual queen to whom this phrase alluded, but because a queen is the highest lady in the land, all virtues are ascribed to her, including possession of all that is complete and thorough. Curiously enough, the expression is American. It first appeared in William Harben's *Abner Daniel* (1902): "You worked 'im to a queen's taste—as fine as spilt milk."

in a pretty pickle

Behind the 8-ball; the devil to pay and no pitch hot; in trouble; in a sorry plight. The Dutch, from whom we borrowed "pickle" and also the original phrase some four or five hundred years ago, said *in de pekel zitten,* literally to sit in the salt liquor used for preserving vegetables and meats. Such a bath, one can well imagine, would not long be comfortable. From time to time through the years our forebears have intensified the expression in such manners as "ill pickle," "sad pickle," "sweet pickle," and nowadays, "pretty pickle."

to walk the plank

To force out of office or position. This refers to a method used in a literal sense for getting rid of undesired persons on shipboard— a method used primarily by pirates or corsairs, especially in the seventeenth century on the Spanish Main, for disposing of unwanted captives in the cheapest, most effective, and least messy way. That is, a plank was laid over the side of the vessel, the captive, hands tied behind, was blindfolded and, by pricks of a dirk or cutlass, compelled to walk along that plank until he fell into the sea.

to play possum

To pretend; to deceive; especially, to feign sickness or death. Early American hunters speedily learned that the opossum is a past master in the art of simulating death. If threatened with capture it will lie with closed eyes and limp muscles, and no amount of handling or ordinary abuse will cause it to show signs of life. Only when thrown into water will it become promptly active. That ability to show every ordinary indication of death gave rise to our expression at least two centuries ago.

as proud as Satan (sin, or Lucifer)

This notion of evil being arrogant, supercilious, or contemptuous arose in the minds of people more than four hundred years ago. The first record in English is in *The Pilgrimage of Perfection* (1526) with "as proude as Nabugodonosor [Nebuchadnezzar]." Then came "as proud as Hell," by Dean Swift in 1711. Then "as proud as Lucifer," by Madame d'Arblay in 1782. And we have since substituted Satan, sin, the devil, Beelzebub, the Prince of Darkness, Old Scratch, Old Harry, or whatever synonym of evil may occur to us.

to take a powder

It is at least interesting to speculate on the origin of a slang phrase, even if there is no possible way of determining who started it nor his line of reasoning. Here we have something meaning to depart rapidly, to flee, to go over the hill, to take it on the lam, to beat it, to dust off or do a dust. It could be, of course, that "flee" suggested "flea," and that powder is used to rid oneself of this pest. But to my notion, "powder" was suggested by "dust" which, in turn, arises from "beating" a carpet, rug, or the like.

to break the ice

To dispel coolness or aloofness; to break through reserve or formality, establish friendly relations; also, to start an enterprise. Literally, of course, it is the ice on a river or lake that is broken for the passage of boats in early spring. Because that denoted the start of the season's activity, it was but natural to connect the expression with the start of an enterprise, and it was thus used almost four centuries ago. The current significance, that of establishing friendly relations, of dispelling reserve, came into general usage through Lord Byron. In *Don Juan* (1823) Canto XIII, referring to the British people, he has the noble don say:

> And your cold people are beyond all price,
> When once you've broken their confounded ice.

hoist with one's own petard

Ruined or destroyed by the device or plot one has set for another; caught in one's own trap. Had it not been for Shakespeare this expression would undoubtedly have died out long ago. It is found in *Hamlet*, one of the most popular of his plays. In Act IV, Polonius, hoping to catch Hamlet in some treasonable utterance in a private conversation with his mother, the queen, has hidden behind an arras in the queen's chamber, but is discovered and slain by Hamlet, who later says, "For tis the sport to haue the enginer Hoise with his owne petar." The "petar," more correctly "petard," was not unlike the modern hand grenade, originally of metal, bell-shaped, charged with powder, and fired by fuse; later, a wooden container. It was used for blowing open a door or making a breach in a wall, and, thanks to poor construction and general ignorance, not uncommonly also blew up the one operating it.

to pile (or heap) Pelion on Ossa

To heap difficulty upon difficulty; to attempt that which is all but impossible. Pelion is a mountain peak in Thessaly, about 5,300 feet high; Ossa, another peak in Thesssaly, about 6,500 feet high. The story is told in Homer's *Odyssey* (Book XI) as follows, according to the Butcher and Lang translation:

And after her I beheld Iphimedeia, . . . and she bare children twain, but short of life were they, godlike Otus and far-famed Ephialtes. Now these were the tallest men that earth, the grain giver, ever reared, and far the goodliest after the renowned Orion. At nine seasons old they were of breadth nine cubits, and nine fathoms in height. They it was who threatened to raise even against the immortals in Olympus the din of stormy war. They strove to pile Ossa on Olympus, and on Ossa Pelion . . . that there might be a pathway to the sky. Yea, and they would have accomplished it, had they reached the full measure of manhood. But the son of Zeus . . . destroyed the twain, ere the down had bloomed beneath their temples, and darkened their chins with the blossom of youth.

come off your perch

Come down a peg or two; don't be too conceited, haughty, or arrogant. The allusion is to the twig serving as a resting place for a bird; hence, a point of vantage from which one may take a superior view. The present expression is American of some fifty years' standing.

to take down a peg

To pull one off his high horse; to knock one off his perch; to humble one; to lower one in his own or another's estimation. This is found as far back as the sixteenth century, but the original allusion has been lost. Shakespeare, in *Love's Labor's Lost* (1592), Act V scene 2, has, "Master, let me take you a button-hole lower," by some interpreted to have the same meaning as our present phrase, but by others as meaning, "Master, let me speak confidentially." Yet "peg" appears at about the same date in the work of debated authorship, *Pappe with an Hatchet* (1589), in lines addressed "To Huffe, Ruffe, etc.," general terms for arrogant bullies: "Now haue at you all my gaffers of the rayling religion, tis I that must take you a peg lower."

It is my surmise that "peg" was originally connected with some game, possibly with one that preceded the introduction of draughts ("checkers" in America) in England, but I have no proof.

neither head nor tail of (a matter)

Neither one thing nor another; nothing definite nor positive: usually in such construction as, I can make neither head nor tail of this story. In the expression, which dates back to the seventeenth century, *head* means "beginning" and *tail* means "end"; hence, I can understand neither beginning nor end of this story.

to keep one's hair on

To restrain one's temper; to remain calm and serene, unruffled despite provocation. This was popular American slang of less than a century ago. In fact, the earliest literary example appears to have been in *Dr. Claudius,* one of the first pieces of fiction written by  Francis Marion Crawford. As with most slang, a positive source of the expression cannot be determined. However, it could have reflected the Indian raids upon isolated homesteaders that were still taking place in some of the western territories. Settlers and wagoners who could remain unexcited in the face of any such raid were the most likely to be able to fight off a threatening horde and thus to retain their scalps. This is, of course, conjecture. Neither Crawford nor other writers of that period, the early 1880's, left any clue that would suggest the source.

Paul Pry

The name is that of the chief character in the play, *Paul Pry,* written in 1825 by John Poole. He was such a perfect exemplar of those who go through life spying and eavesdropping into the affairs of others that the name was speedily adopted into the language. *Brewer's Handbook* (edition of 1898) thus defines the character: "an idle, inquisitive, meddlesome fellow, who has no occupation of his own, and is for ever poking his nose into other people's affairs. He always comes in with the apology, 'I hope I don't intrude.' "

to dislike (or like) the cut of one's jib

To dislike, or be chary of, the appearance of a person, or his character; to have a feeling of distrust. (Only occasionally do we use the opposite, "like.") The saying arose from nautical terminology of the seventeenth century, when the jib—the large triangular sail stretching forward from top and bottom of the foremast to the outer end of the boom, or to the bowsprit—was introduced on sailing vessels. Certain characteristic shapes of this jib served, among sailors, to identify the nationality of a vessel, and, therefore, whether the vessel might be friendly or hostile. But it was not, however, until the early nineteenth century that Southey, Walter Scott, Marryat, and others began to give the phrase its modern meaning.

in the lap (or on the knees) of the gods

According to the will of the gods; in the hands of fate or Providence; beyond one's control. The origin is Greek; the earliest occurrence is found in Homer's *Iliad*, Book XVII, line 514. The speaker was Automedon, and the occasion was the fight over the body of the slain Patroclos, friend and companion of Achilles. The Trojans, led by Hector, had already stripped the body of its armor, armor lent by Achilles to Patroclos, and, to disgrace the Acheans further, sought to drag the corpse away, intending to cut off the head, carry it in triumph into the city, and throw the body to the dogs. It was at this juncture that Automedon, watching the ebb and flow of battle, said, "All is in the lap of the gods," or, as some translate it, "on the knees of the gods." But the threat of disgrace did serve, however, to bring about a reconciliation between the powerful Achilles and Agamemnon, leader of the Acheans, and to induce Achilles to re-enter the war, eventually to rout the Trojans and slay his arch-enemy, Hector.

to get one's monkey up

To get one's dander up; to become angry. Apparently, along about a hundred years ago, people first began to compare their sudden fits of anger with the unreasoning bursts of rage so often seen among members of the simian family. The expression is of British origin and, though sometimes heard on the western side of the Atlantic, is generally confined to the place of its origin.

ish kabibble

That, at least, is the usual way the expression appears. Some, however, write it as a solid word, *ishkabibble,* and others make it three words, *ish ka bibble.* Actually you may spell it as you wish, for, like the Missouri mule, it has no pride of ancestry and no hope of posterity. Its source, that is, is unknown. It sprang into popularity roughly about 1915, and was long thought to be a Yiddish phrase equivalent to "I should worry"—meaning "it is of no concern to me"—which came into vogue at about the same time. But the Jews disclaim the saying. In fact, the usual Yiddish expression is, *Es is mein daige,* "It is my worry."

drunk as a fiddler

Highly intoxicated; three sheets in the wind; squiffy; spifflicated; tanked. It would be quite an achievement to be able to prove that the "fiddler" in the case was Nero, who, somewhat shellacked himself at the time presumably, fiddled while Rome burned, during his  reign back in the first century, but alas, this is just one of a variety of men of trades or position who, proverbially, or in fact, have been guzzlers. Others through the centuries have been, drunk as a beggar, as a lord, a piper, tinker, emperor, and fool, and there have also been "rattes," back in the sixteenth century, and a wheelbarrow in the eighteenth, as well as a fish, a "mous," "swyn," ape, and owl. The "fiddler" has prevailed, and with the best of reasons. The fiddler, always presumed to be well pleased with a chance to play, has had to be content with meager pay. In times past it was proverbial that "fiddler's pay" was nothing more than thanks and all the wine he could drink, and even when the thanks did include a few pence, the wine was supposed to make up for its scantness. What could he do but get drunk?

biggest frog (toad) in the puddle

The person of most importance in any community or group. The group or community is always a small one, otherwise the person would be a personage and "the biggest fish in the sea." Daddy is,

usually, the biggest frog in a domestic puddle, especially if he wears the pants of the family, but in a small community the relatively important individual—and rarely does that importance spread beyond the community—may be the banker, the police chief, the preacher, or the boss politician. He is, at any rate, the one to whom everyone kowtows. He's the one making the loudest "kerchunk." We've had this Americanism for at least seventy-five years.

dark horse

Originally this was a racing term for a horse about which nothing was known; its abilities had been kept "in the dark"—secret, that is—until it appeared on the track. Benjamin Disraeli is credited with the first literary usage in that sense in *The Young Duke* (1831): "A dark horse, which had never been thought of . . . rushed past the grand stand in sweeping triumph." Though a recent anonymous newspaper columnist attributes the origin to a "dark colored horse named 'Dusty Pete' " owned by a Tennessean, "Sam Flynn," who "used to ride from town to town" entering the horse, which appeared to be lame, in local races and snapping up the money, the story is another instance of folk etymology. Disraeli, both before and after entering the British political arena, was a popular writer, accepted in America as in England. Accordingly, when, to break the deadlock in the Democratic convention of 1844 among the adherents of Van Buren, Lewis Cass, and James Buchanan, the name of James K. Polk was introduced on the ninth ballot, he was the "dark horse" that had not been thought of—and this was the actual introduction of the term into political usage.

to add insult to injury

To heap scorn upon one already injured. Apperson, in *English Proverbs and Proverbial Phrases* (1929), reports that this familiar expression first appeared in Latin—*iniuriae qui addideris contumeliam,* "injury which is added to insult"—in the fifth book of the fables written by the Roman writer of the first century, A.D., Phaedrùs. But we probably owe our acquaintance with it from its use by Dickens in *Pickwick Papers*: ' To offer me a sandwich, when I am looking for a supper, is to add insult to injury."

to stick (or stand) to one's guns

To persevere in one's course despite obstacles; to hold out for, or insist on, a desired course; to maintain one's position. Obviously, the origin is military, pertaining to any commander who is determined to maintain a present position in the face of heavy attack by an enemy. As such, it could have been said of any determined leader since the invention of the gun. Curiously, however, our figurative usage traces back little more than a century, the earliest being found in Samuel Warren's popular farcical novel, *Ten Thousand a Year* (1839), in which the timorous character, Mr. Titmouse, in an argument, "though greatly alarmed," is said to have "stood to his gun pretty steadily."

to go up in the air

This is said not only of balloons and aviators, but of ordinary persons, American fathers especially, who become vociferously enraged, who sputter furiously in resemblance to a skyrocket with an ignited fuse, from which the expression originated some fifty or sixty years ago. Its British equivalent is "to get one's monkey up," which arose from the readiness with which the short-lived ire of monkeys is aroused.

on the water cart (or wagon)

The watering or sprinkling cart was a much more familiar vehicle on our dusty American streets a few decades ago than it is today. In fact, nowadays one sees only a motorized version of it cooling hot paved city streets in midsummer. But from the use of this former vehicle in slaking the dust of the roads, those of our forebears, troubled with dusty throats but seeking to avoid strong drink, spoke of climbing aboard the water cart. The expression arose during the heyday of the Prohibition movement, in the 1890's. The earliest record cited in *The Dictionary of Americanisms* is that appearing in Alice Caldwell Rice's *Mrs. Wiggs of the Cabbage Patch* (1901). Mrs. Wiggs, speaking of Mr. Dick, who is "consumpted," said: "He coughs all the time, jes' like Mr. Wiggs done. Other day he had a orful spell while I was there. I wanted to git him some whisky, but he shuck his head, 'I'm on the water-cart,' sez he."

to bite the dust (or ground or sand)

In America it is always dust that the hated villain or redskin bites when slain in mortal combat; in England, ground or sand. However, it is merely a matter of translation, for the original picturesque phrase is to be found in Homer's *Iliad,* Book II, lines 417–18. This, in the almost literal translation of William Cowper (1838), Vol. I, page 49, reads: ". . . his friends, around him, prone in dust, shall bite the ground." Whereas the American poet, William Cullen Bryant (1870), Vol. I, Book II, lines 514–15, gives it: ". . . his fellow warriors, many a one, Fall round him to the earth and bite the dust." But earlier than Bryant to use the favorite American idiom was the British explorer in South Africa, Carl J. Andersson. In his *Lake Ngami* (1856), page 363, he tells of a hunter who "had made numerous lions bite the dust." Regrettably the expression, from overuse, is losing its punch. Modern slang has now so greatly reduced its force that it implies little more than to suffer disaster of moderate degree. A horseman "bites the dust" if he falls or is thrown; a boxer, if he is knocked down or knocked out; a businessman, if he fails.

beside the mark

This is very old. In fact, it is so old that, in the original **Greek**, it had passed from a proverbial phrase into a single word which expressed its figurative sense. That is, in the old Athenian contests, an archer who failed to hit the mark was said to be out of the lists or course; hence, beside the mark. The same thing, though in English, was said of the English bowman—sometimes by variation, "far from the mark," "wide of the mark," "short of the mark," "to miss the mark." The Greek single word, which may be represented by roman type as *exagonion,* had the figurative meaning, "irrelevant; not pertinent," precisely the meaning we give to the English phrase.

hocus-pocus

Flimflam; deception; deceit; nonsense; charlatanism; jugglery: sometimes corrupted to "hokey-pokey." Probably this was originally a form of reduplication—like hodgepodge, odd-bods, shilly-shally, and many others—and was based on Latin. One explanation is given in 1656 by Thomas Ady in *A Candle in the Dark; or, A Treatise Concerning the Nature of Witches and Witchcraft*: "I will speake of one man . . that went about in King James his time . . who called himself, The Kings Majesties most excellent Hocus Pocus, and so was called, because that at the playing of every Trick, he used to say, *Hocus pocus, tontus talontus, vade celeriter jubeo,* a dark composure of words, to blinde the eyes of the beholders, to make his Trick pass the more currantly without discovery." Whether from that conjurer or not is not certain, but early in that century—just as one magician or one boxer today adopts the name of a successful predecessor—the name Hocus Pocus, Hocas Pocas, Hokos Pokos, or the like was bestowed upon any juggler or conjuror.

to make one's hair stand on end

To frighten or terrify; to cause one to become rigid with fear; to scare the pants off one. This might almost pass as a literal condition, because when one is suddenly terrified the hair on one's head tends to rise, or feels as if it does, like the fur of a cat or the mane of a dog. Even a baldheaded man feels a prickling of the scalp from a sudden terror or fright. Undoubtedly the condition was recognized in early days, but the earliest English record is not found before 1530. Occurring in John Palsgrave's *Lesclarcissement de la Langue Françoyse* it may be, in fact, a translation of the French, *faire dresser les cheveux*, "to make the hair stand erect." But Palsgrave's line is: "When I passed by the churche yarde my heares stode upright for feare." Thereafter many writers took the metaphor to their bosom.

to be well heeled

In these days one is well heeled who has plenty of money, is well fixed or well-to-do, just the opposite of one who is down at the heels. Since the latter—down at the heels—alludes directly to the usual run-down condition of the shoeheels of one who is hard-pressed for money, it might be supposed that well heeled originally alluded to the reverse condition. But that is not the case. Originally, back in the eighteenth century, it was a game cock that was well heeled; that is, provided with a good "heel" or artificial spur before it faced an opponent in the pit. From that, in the United States, men began to "heel" themselves, to arm themselves with gun or pistol, before entering a zone in which trouble might be expected. If well armed, they were "well heeled," from the troubled days in the West, and in the South following the War between the States. Hence, perhaps because most troubles can be alleviated by money, the expression soon took on its present financial aspect.

to make a mountain (out) of a molehill

To make a great to-do over a trifle; to give something far greater importance than is justified. This is by no means a new idea. In fact, as dug up by Apperson, you will find that the witty Greek writer, Lucian (A.D. 125?–210?), used it in his "Ode to a Fly": "to make an elephant of a fly." This has passed into a French proverb of identical meaning, *faire d'une mouche un éléphant*, as well as into the German *aus einer Mucke einen Elefanten machen*. Just why the Greek saying did not pass by direct translation into English is something to be guessed at, but instead, about four hundred years ago the elephant became a mountain, and the fly, gnat, or flyspeck became a molehile. It is first found in *Foxe's Book of Martyrs* (1570): "To much amplifying things yᵗ be but small, makyng mountaines of Molehils."

handwriting on the wall

A forecast of some ominous event; a warning of probable danger. The allusion is to the account told in the fifth chapter of Daniel in the Old Testament. Belshazzar, to celebrate his access to the throne of Babylonia upon the death of his father, Nebuchadnezzar, declared a great feast, and, to signify the complete subjugation of the Jews, had the golden vessels that were taken out of the temple at Jerusalem brought out, "and the king, and his princes, his wives, and his concubines drank in them." At this sacrilege, "came forth fingers of a man's hand, and wrote over against the candlestick upon the plaster of the wall." The words written were, *"Mene, mene, tekel, upharsin."* The king demanded of Daniel, the Jewish prophet, an interpretation, and was told: "This is the interpretation of the thing: *Mene*; God hath numbered thy kingdom, and finished it. *Tekel*; Thou art weighed in the balances, and art found wanting. *Peres*; Thy kingdom is divided, and given to the Medes and Persians." The chapter closes: "In that night was Belshazzar the king of the Chaldeans slain. And Darius the Median took the kingdom."

in one ear and out the other

Through the mind, but leaving no impression; as though a sound traveled through a tube passing through the skull leaving no evidence of its passing. The notion is by no means new; probably

Adam gave utterance to something similar after giving some instruction to Cain and Abel. But the earliest English record concerned a sermon "upon Deuteronomie" by John Calvin which, according to his English translator, Arthur Golding in 1583, "goes in at the one eare and out at the other." There is little doubt but that many another sermon has shared the same reaction in the four centuries since.

like Hogan's goat

Poor old Hogan is merely an innocent bystander in this modern Americanism. Just as with "Hogan's brickyard," a slang designation of a baseball diamond, the goat could be the property of Jones, Smith, or Rockefeller, or VanTassel. That is, the name of the owner has no bearing whatever on the meaning of the expression. When one says that a given TV show, movie, book, or whatever is "like Hogan's goat," he is just with reasonable politeness saying that "it stinks terrifically."

playing to the grandstand (or gallery)

A contributor (David Shulman) to *American Speech* dug up a neat early description of the first expression, which he found in Thomas W. Lawton's *The Krank: His Language and What It Means* (1888): "Playing to the Grand-Stand. To accomplish this it is only necessary to smile, strike an attitude—and strike out." That is too often true, not only in baseball, as Lawton gives it, but in any sport or stage endeavor or whatever in which the performer strives or appears to strive to win the plaudits of the spectators, to show off his self-acclaimed marvelous skill or ability, especially to those he wishes to impress in the near-by high-priced grandstand seats. But one who attempts a grandstand-play, as we call it, must be very sure that he can carry it through, otherwise he may fall flat on his face and meet with hoots of derision. The earlier saying, "playing to the gallery," is still very much in use. Originally it had reference to those actors, especially in an English theater, who, going over the heads of the near-by, and frequently inattentive, occupants of orchestra seats or stalls, deliberately overacted their roles in seeking to gain the approval of the larger populace in the gallery. One had to shout and strike exaggerated attitudes and employ exaggerated gestures, just as the street orator, senator, or M.P. does today who is addressing his remarks primarily to the "dear peepul."

mad as a hatter

This doesn't mean irate, a sense one sometimes hears; it means crazy, utterly demented. There have been various theories advanced for this peculiar metaphor, and some of the theories are themselves peculiar. One is that "hatter" was introduced merely to add an intensive force, that the individual spoken of was just more "mad" than would be ordinarily expected under the circumstances. Another is that the original comparison was "mad as an adder," under the assumption, I suppose, that adders are always insane. But an explanation that I like was that given in an issue (Vol. 155, No. 3) of *The Journal of the American Medical Association*: "It seems that mercury is used in the making of felt hats. Often the unfortunate hatter who would work for years with the mercury would be afflicted with a violent and uncontrollable twitching of his muscles as a result of its poisoning effects. His friends, not understanding the cause of his strange gyrations, concluded that he was mad." Lewis Carroll's character, "The Mad Hatter," in *Alice in Wonderland* (1865) was derived from the expression, but it was in use by Thomas Haliburton in 1837 in *The Clockmaker,* and because mercury was used in hat-making much earlier than that, it may have already been in the argot of hatters long previously.

putting on the dog

Making pretensions of grandeur; assuming airs. This was American college slang of the 1860's. Whether or not it originated at Yale, it was so credited by Lyman H. Bagg who, in his *Four Years at Yale* (1871), wrote: "*Dog,* style, splurge. To put on dog is to make a flashy display, to cut a swell"—and the latter expression in the definition could be defined, "to appear important." The source of college slang even of today can be little more than guesswork, and to go back eighty-five years is necessarily conjectural. But it was then that the Blenheim and the King Charles spaniels were at the height of aristocratic popularity. Nothing could appear snootier, more high-toned than those dogs. Perhaps we owe this doggy phrase to them.

to pay the piper

To pay the fiddler; to settle the score; hence, to suffer the consequences; to take one's punishment, face the music, or take the rap. This had the same allusion as "to pay the fiddler"; that is, to pay the musician who led a dance, and the piper was one of the earliest to supply such music. Incidentally, until well into the nineteenth century, all such musicians, like the itinerant minstrels of earlier days, were considered to be scarcely a step above domestic menials. Hence, any pay they were given, beyond food and all the wine they could drink, was through the bounty of the master of the house.

a gone goose (or **beaver, chick,** etc.)

In *A Hog on Ice,* page 92, I repeated a couple of amusing but legendary yarns that might account for the expression "a gone coon," but I have been reminded that the coon is but one of various specimens of animal life which, in American speech, have and are similarly "gone" or hopelessly done for. "*A gone goose*" dates from 1830; "*a gone chick*" from 1834; "*a gone beaver*" from 1848; "*a gone horse*" from 1840; "*a gone gander*" from 1848, and James K. Paulding, in *Westward Ho!* (1832), even gave us "*gone suckers.*" But there are no legends to account for the hopeless state in which these creatures found themselves.

a Roland for an Oliver

Tit for tat; a blow for a blow; an eye for an eye. There was an actual Roland, a knight who fought under Charlemagne and who was killed in a rear-guard action in the Pyrenees in A.D. 778. From his heroic action grew the famous medieval *Chanson de Roland* (*Ballad of Roland*) and other legends that spread into all parts of Europe.

In one popular form the story was of a most romantic friendship between Roland and one of his companions, Oliver, who was the equal of Roland in every respect. They remind one of the Bobbsey twins. Whatever one could do, the other could do with precisely the same ability. Eventually the two engaged in a combat which, though fought for five days, ended in a tie. In some accounts, both were killed in the action in the Pyrenees, Roland by an accidental

90 ·

blow by his friend Oliver, who had himself received a fatal wound. Thus the two remained equal in death. Because of the various monumental deeds accredited to the two heroes, the saying is also sometimes employed to mean one tall tale to match another.

gosh all hemlock!

This is just one of various minced oaths or ejaculations by which a man who thinks he is nonprofane actually says "God Almighty!" *Gosh* has served as a substitute for "God"—usually in "By gosh"—for more than two hundred years. Some other similar substitutes that have appeared on the American literary scene are, gosh-a-mighty, gosh awful, gosh burned, and even, back in 1857, gosh all Potomac.

to have the goods on one

To catch one with the goods, or, that is to say, to have evidence or proof of one's guilt; to catch one red-handed. "Goods" in such usage refers to merchandise of any sort, whatever article a thief may purloin. The American expression dates from about the turn of the present century.

to warm the cockles of one's heart

To evoke a glow of pleasure in one; to produce a feeling of friendliness, affection, sympathy, or the like in one. Considering the fact that the study of anatomy—most other studies too, for that matter—was stagnant throughout the Dark Ages, or roughly from the time of Galen in the second century to that of Vesalius in the sixteenth, it is astonishing that anatomists of the seventeenth century were already likening the human heart to the shape and valves of the mollusk, common on European shores, and the cockle. That is to say, they saw sufficient resemblance between the two valves of the mollusk and the two ventricles of the heart to refer to the latter as the cockles. Thus, because the heart was long supposed to be the seat of the affections, men spoke of delighting, of rejoicing, of pleasing, and, more recently, of warming the cockles of one's heart.

to be a piker

To be a cheap-skate, tin-horn gambler, four-flusher, etc.; to be a poor sport or small better. Although this American term is less than a hundred years old, its origin is shrouded in uncertainty. It could have been derived from a regiment, commanded by Colonel Zebulon M. Pike in the War of 1812, so poorly armed that many of the men drilled with pikes instead of bayonets. Or it could have derived from the denizens of Pike County, Missouri (also named from Z. M. Pike), who, among the Forty-Niners of California, were called Pikes, Pikies, or pikers, any of which designated worthless, lazy, good-for-nothing persons. Or, in my own opinion it may have derived from a vagrant or tramp who, lacking means for other transportation, traveled on shank's mare—afoot, that is—down the pike; a foot traveler on the pike.

Barmecide feast (or banquet)

This comes from the "Story of the Barber's Sixth Brother" in *Arabian Nights*. A poor beggar, Schacabac, without food for several days, asked for bread at the door of the rich Persian noble, Barmecide. To his amazement he was invited to the table. Servants brought  golden platter after golden platter, and his host urged him to help himself freely But there was not a thing upon any of the platters. Nevertheless the beggar entered into the spirit of the jest, pretended to pile his plate full and to eat bountifully, and when, at the end of the repast, an empty jug of wine was brought, Schacabac pretended to fill and refill his goblet frequently and, eventually, to become quite drunk. In this feigned state he boxed his host heartily on the ears. This and the good nature of the beggar so delighted Barmecide that he then had a real banquet brought to the table. Thus, nowadays, a *Barmecide* is one who offers an unreal or disappointing benefit, and a *Barmecide feast* or *banquet* is a meal that, however inviting to the eye, fails to live up to expectations.

Shangri-la

A place of mystery; utopia. The place was fictional, some mysterious region in Tibet conceived by the late English-born novelist, James Hilton, in *Lost Horizon* (1933), where people lived for hundreds of years and attempted to preserve the best achievements in art and ideals of the outside world despite its tensions. The concept gained widespread appeal. Thus when, in World War II, President F. D. Roosevelt smilingly told reporters that the flyers under General James Doolittle in the bombing of Tokyo had taken off from Shangri-la, it was immediately understood that the point of departure was not to be made public, was to remain as undisclosed as Hilton's place of mystery.

Sam Hill

After long and diligent search for some American of sufficient prominence in a bygone generation to justify the continued use of his name, even to the present time, in such sayings as "to run like Sam Hill," "What the Sam Hill," "Who the Sam Hill," and so on, I have come to the reluctant conclusion that the editors of *The Dictionary of Americanisms* were right in calling the term "a euphemism for *hell.*" It may be, as Edwin V. Mitchell says in his *Encyclopedia of American Politics* (1946), that there was a Colonel Samuel Hill of Guilford, Connecticut, who continuously ran for and was elected to public office in both town and state, but this colonel, though perhaps locally prominent, does not turn up in any of the numerous biographical records I have consulted. Nor does Mr. Mitchell supply any dates. The expression itself had sufficiently widespread usage to extend into Schuyler County, New York, by 1839.

right as a trivet

Absolutely right; right as rain; all hunkydory; all to the mustard. Inasmuch as a trivet, a stand for supporting vessels in a fireplace, was always three-legged in former times, the housewife could set it anywhere upon her hearth, certain that a pot thereon would rest securely. The expression began to appear in literature early in the nineteenth century.

to go to rack (or wrack) and ruin

To go to destruction; go to pot; go haywire; go to the dogs. In the sixteenth century, and later, men spelled by ear, rather than through knowledge of the historical background of words. In fact, many of our present-day spellings are still affected by that custom. *Rack*, in this phrase, is one of them. It should have been, and should now be, *wrack*, which in turn was another spelling of *wreck* and with the same meaning. But we have had "rack and ruin" almost four hundred years and in the works of the best writers, even to the present day, and a change would be a slow process.

on the rocks

As used in American slang this respected and well-established phrase has taken on a variety of interpretations. They all relate to some form or another of dilapidation or ruin, however. Thus a person "on the rocks" may be ruined financially or "busted"; or he may be suffering a physical or mental collapse or "off his hinges," "minus some buttons," "gone haywire." A marriage "on the rocks" is one that is about to be, or has been, broken up. A business or other venture "on the rocks" has failed or, at least, is in a desperate plight. Figurative use in the sense of being destitute dates back some two hundred years, and was derived from the literal nautical sense of the condition of a vessel shipwrecked on a rocky coast.

to scare the daylights out of (a person)

To frighten extremely; to alarm intensely; to make one's hair stand on end; to scare stiff. The daylights here differ from those in the common saying, "to let daylight into a person." In that, the meaning is "light"—to make a hole in a person big enough for light to enter. But here, daylight means wits; hence, to scare a person witless. In my own span of life someone—at first, one or another of my brothers—has tried to scare the daylights out of me from the time I was two, and I'm sure the expression is just as well known and has been as long used in many another American family. Some people amplify it to "the living daylights," but it adds up to the same thing. However, the recorders of the language have heretofore missed this expression.

sacred cow

Any personal possessions cherished by its owner, or a person held in such high esteem or of such high office as to be above criticism or attack, someone on a pedestal. This twentieth-century term could have been derived from the cow, held to be sacred in India even at the present time, from the legendary hero, Prithu who assumed the form of a cow in order to encourage his subjects to raise edible vegetables. Or it could have been taken from Greek legend, the story of Io who was transformed into a heifer because Zeus had become too amorous. Or it could have had reference to the Egyptian Hathor, goddess of love, who, in the form of a cow, was served by princesses. Perhaps, even, it is somehow connected with the ejaculation "Holy cow!" made familiar in the 1940's to thousands of American radio listeners as the pet oath of "Oogie," boy friend of Corliss Archer. Most probably, however, the connection is with the sacred cow of India.

Indian sign

Evidently Frederick Webb Hodge, editor of the *Handbook of American Indians* (1907), issued by the Smithsonian Institution and still regarded as the leading authority on Indian life and customs, did not foresee that movies, radio, and television would perpetuate—at least, among children—an interest in those first inhabitants of the continent. On the meaning of this term he says merely: "A Western colloquialism of the earlier settlement days for a trace of the recent presence of Indians." It is no longer a colloquialism, nor is it confined to the West, nor to early settlement days. But Hodge missed an expression familiarly used in my boyhood—"to put (or hang) the Injun sign on someone." By that we meant, to mark a person for injury or for defeat in a contest; to put a jinx on one; to wish him ill luck.

taken to the cleaners

Defrauded; despoiled; mulcted; flimflammed; stung; played for a sucker; also punished or severely defeated. This is merely a modernized form of the slang term "cleaned out," used by some of our great-grandfathers in the early nineteenth century. The *New and*

Comprehensive Vocabulary of the Flash Language, written in 1812 by James H. Vaux, defined the older phrase: "Said of a gambler who lost his last stake at play; also, of a flat [dupe] who has been stript of all his money." The modern form, however, introduces a subtle play on words in the secondary meanings of punished or defeated in the suggestion that he who has been cleaned has been sent through a washing machine or has been subjected to the machinations of a dry-cleaning establishment.

to knock on wood

Why do even those among us who loudly proclaim utter freedom from superstition feel just a bit reluctant to state that such-and-such calamity has never happened without immediately feeling an urge to tap on some solid piece of wood? As everyone knows, the act is supposed to avert evil or misfortune which otherwise might attend vainglorious speech.

No one knows how the superstition arose, but George Stimpson, in *A Book about a Thousand Things* (1946), which the publishers, Harper & Brothers, permit me to quote, presents some of the numerous theories that have been offered. He says:

. . . Some attribute it to the old game known as "touching wood" or "wood tag," in which a player who succeeds in touching wood is safe from capture. Others hold that this game and "knocking on wood" had a common origin in primitive tree worship, when trees were believed to harbor protective spirits. To rap on a tree—the dwelling place of a friendly spirit—was to call up the spirit of the tree to protect one against impending misfortune. Later, people would place the hand on a wooden statue of a deity for the same purpose. It is said that among certain European peasants it is still common to knock loudly on wood to keep away evil spirits. Still others believe the superstition is of Christian origin and that it is in some way associated with the wooden cross upon which Jesus was crucified. Perhaps, they think, it is a survival of the religious rite of touching a crucifix when taking an oath or the beads of the rosary when praying.

a drop in the bucket (or sea, or ocean)

Any quantity far too small; a smithereen. The metaphor first appeared in the English translation of the Bible by John Wyclif

(1382) in Isaiah ix, 15: "Lo! Jentiles as a drope of a boket, and as moment of a balaunce ben holden." In the King James version the passage reads: "Behold, the nations are as a drop of a bucket, and are counted as the small dust of the balance." Charles Dickens gave impetus to the further alteration or expansion in *A Christmas Carol* (1844). In the first conversation between Scrooge and the ghost of his deceased partner, Marley, the ghost says: "The dealings of my trade were but a drop of water in the comprehensive ocean of my business." And nowadays the "drop" may be of any liquid into any proportionately great body.

to be in a hole

To be in debt; hence, in difficulty or trouble; in a predicament; on the spot; with one's back to the wall. The "hole" here is not the same one as that, in a poker game, in which one may have an ace in the hole, though this too is said to have had its origin at the poker table. That is, so says John P. Quinn in *Fools of Fortune* (1892), the proprietors of a gambling joint take a certain percentage out of the pot on each hand called as the amount due the house; "a pair of aces and another pair, and you must 'go to the hole' with a check. The 'hole' is a slot cut in the middle of the poker table, leading to a locked drawer underneath, and all checks deposited therein are the property of the keeper of the place."

to trip the light fantastic

To dance. In full, the expression is "to trip the light fantastic toe." It comes from John Milton's "L'Allegro" (1632), from the early lines beginning:

> Haste thee Nymph and bring with thee
> Jest and youthful Jollity,

and going on to—

> Sport that wrinkled Care derides,
> And Laughter holding both his sides.
> Come, and trip it as ye go
> On the light fantastick toe.

to be in the same boat

Obviously, two or more people or things occupying one boat must share equal risks, and the phrase has thus acquired such figurative meaning; to share risks equally, to have identical obligations or involvements, to be in or live under similar conditions. Literary usage of the phrase goes back only about a hundred years, but it may have had its origin in an older expression, by three centuries, "to have an oar in another's boat," that is, to interfere in or meddle with the affairs of another.

to take one's Bible oath

To be absolutely certain; to have no shadow of doubt. Alluding to the oath that one takes as a witness in a court, in which, under certain circumstances, one places his right hand upon the Bible or holds it, or the New Testament, in his right hand and swears "to tell the truth, the whole truth, and nothing but the truth; so help me God." Accordingly, an expression of willingness "to take one's Bible oath" is a statement that one is willing to enter such a court and to swear such an oath. Alas, unfortunately the statement is often, if not usually, that of a scoundrel, to whom the sanctity of the Bible or of such an oath is meaningless. The expression is criminal slang, and usage seems to have started in the past half century.

to hem and haw

To express hesitancy or uncertainty; sometimes to express a qualified disapproval. Actually we have made a compound verb out of two vocal sounds by which we ordinarily express such hesitance. That is, we "hem" when we clear the throat with a slight vocal effort, as if about to speak; we "haw," originally "hawk," when we clear the throat with greater effort. Back in 1580, in Gervase Babington's *A Profitable Exposition of the Lord's Prayer,* we find, "Wee gape and we yawne, we hem and we hawke." A century earlier, however, in one of the *Paston Letters* written in 1469, we find: "He wold have gotyn it aweye by humys [hums] and by hays [ha's or haws], but I wold not so be answeryd." Shakespeare, as did some other writers of the seventeenth century, used "hum and ha."

touch and go

An uncertain, risky, or precarious state of things, a narrow escape; also, an immediate or rapid action. The expression arose in the early years of the past century, and both interpretations were in vogue from the beginning, probably because any narrow escape is averted through immediate or rapid action. For the origin, probably Admiral William H. Smyth was right in his definition of the term in *The Sailor's Word-book* (1865): "Said of anything within an ace of ruin; as in rounding a ship very narrowly to escape rocks, &c, or when, under sail, she rubs against the ground with her keel, without much diminution of her velocity."

Tom-and-Jerry

Nowadays this is a drink, one composed of brandy, rum, beaten egg, sugar, nutmeg, and hot milk or water. These components may vary somewhat, but those are the usual current ingredients in the United States. The name is derived from two characters in Pierce Egan's *Life in London; or, Days and Nights of Jerry Hawthorne and his Elegant Friend Corinthian Tom* (1821). This book, describing the sporting activities of that day, illustrated by George Cruikshank, was immensely popular. Hence, through the earlier "Jerry shop," a term for a low beer hall, the two names, *Tom* and *Jerry*, in this reversed order, began to be associated with drinking and carousing within a few years after the appearance of the book. A standard recipe for the drink, however—by one under the nom de plume, Jerry Thomas—did not appear until 1862.

on tick

On credit. Years ago, when this commercial term first came into use, it indicated a written document, a form of IOU. That is, it was just a contraction of "on ticket," and the "ticket" was some form of note of hand, or acknowledgment of indebtedness. The contracted form came into use in the fore part of the seventeenth century. *The Oxford English Dictionary* cites a usage of 1642: "They would haue . . run on tick with Piggin for inke and songs, rather than haue lost the show of your presence."

Tom, Dick, and Harry

This group of names signifying any indiscriminate collection of masculine representatives of *hoi polloi* was a more or less haphazard choice. It probably started with names common in the sixteenth century. Thus Sir David Lyndesay, in *Ane Dialog betwix Experience and ane Courteour* (*c.* 1555), has, "Wherefore to colliers, carters and cokes to Iack [Jack] and Tom my rime shall be directed." And Shakespeare, in *Love's Labour's Lost* (1588), gives us in the closing song, "And Dicke the Shepheard blowes his nails; and Tom beares Logges into the hall." And "Dick, Tom, and Jack" served through the seventeenth century. But our present group was apparently an American selection. It appeared (according to George L. Kittredge's *The Old Farmer and His Almanac,* 1904) in *The Farmer's Almanack* for 1815: "So he hired Tom, Dick and Harry, and at it they went."

with the tail between the legs

That's Fido for you. Put him up against a toy terrier half his size and his tail promptly turns down under his belly. Maybe he'll even turn on his back, all four legs limp. Brave dog! The attitude of a cowardly or scared dog is so typical that we have long said of a thoroughly cowed, utterly abased, or dejected person that he stands or runs "with his tail between his legs."

to take (something) lying down

Usually the "something" is an insult or act of scorn, contempt, derision, or the like that we do *not* take, or intend to take, with the submission implied by recumbency—passively, that is. In fact, he who does "take it lying down" is likely to be regarded as spineless, or perhaps as a bootlicker, stooge, apple-polisher, or toady. It is an American expression, perhaps twenty-five or thirty years old.

100 ·

to play ball with one

To coöperate with one; to accept as a fellow; also, sometimes to accept as a friend or a confidant. In its literal sense the expression first alluded to the necessity for each member of a ball team—baseball or football—to coöperate with all other members in all possible ways during any game in order to play most effectively. From an admonition by the coaches of successful teams, the expression extended into social and commercial usage in the 1920's.

on Easy Street

Having an easy living; in comfortable circumstances; prosperous; riding on the gravy train. American slang from the close of the nineteenth century. The earliest record of this imaginary street in the *Dictionary of American English* takes it to George V. Hobart's *It's Up to You* (1902), in which the author tells of a young man "who could walk up and down Easy Street."

to swear like a trooper

To swear tremendous oaths; to use extreme profanity. Some anonymous newspaper columnist, recently, though using *trouper* instead of *trooper*, said, "This expression started and was used in church meetings as late as the 1900's. The troupers referred to are stage actors and the saying was used to denote the low esteem show people were regarded by many people." Sorry, but, except possibly for the lack of esteem in which actors were held by some unfortunate people, the statement is altogether untrue. The expression is at least a hundred and fifty years old, and the reference is to the habit of strong profanity among British cavalrymen at that period.

to cut a (big) swath

This was slang, back in the 1840's. It alluded to the wide sweep of grass mown by a scythe; hence, to the flourish made by a pompous person swaggering down the walk. In fact, the first literary use of this American slang was precisely that. It was in *High Life in New York* (1843), by Ann Stephens: "Gracious me! how he was strutting up the side-walk—didn't he cut a swath!" The popular creator of the fictional character, Sam Slick, undoubtedly helped

perpetuate the phrase. In *Nature and Human Nature* (1855), that
is, Thomas C. Haliburton had the lines, "The Miss A——s cut a
tall swathe, I tell you, for they say they are descended from a governor of Nova Scotia, and that their relatiōns in England are some
punkins too."

to make hay while the sun shines

Since hay is the resultant of mown grass dried for fodder, and
the sun is the cheapest and most available drying agency, the literal
sense of this aphorism is most obvious. Its figurative intent is
equivalent to "Strike while the iron is hot," and in fact such are
both the German and French phrases: *Das Eisen schmieden
solange es noch heiss ist,* and *Battre le fer pendant qu'il est chaud.*
That is, the English phrase means, if an explanation is needed, to
seize opportunity by the forelock; to take advantage of a good thing
before it slips past. John Heywood in his *All the Prouerbes in the
Englishe Tongue* (1546) gave it: "Whan the sunne shinth make
hay."

to splice the mainbrace

Either literally or figuratively this required the full crew of a sailing vessel. The mainbrace is the rope by which the mainsail is
trimmed. To splice this rope requires the services of the entire crew,
and at the conclusion of this arduous task it became the custom
in the British Navy, in days of sail, to serve rum to all hands. From
that custom, "to splice the mainbrace" became the accepted naval
term in the early nineteenth century as a call to serve grog, a call
speedily adopted among landlubbers and still in use by them,
though long dropped in nautical lingo.

to knock the spots off one

Just what these spots were, which when knocked off gave one
a victory, is a matter of guess. Apparently they were New England
spots, and possibly localized still further in Vermont. At least the
first printed reference leads to the latter inference. It was in an article on the breeding of Morgan horses in the publication, *Porter's
Spirit of the Times*, November 22, 1856: "Addison County leads

the van (or 'knocks the spots off,' as we say here) in Vermont and is celebrated over the world for its fine horses." I have a hunch that the "spots" were the prominent members of the countenance of one's adversary, the eyes, the nose, at which one would be most likely to aim one's fists.

to sing another (or a different) tune, or, to change one's tune

To speak or act in a different manner; to assume a different attitude; to change the subject, or, especially, to humble oneself. The school bully sings a different tune after brave Johnny, finally stirred to anger, gives him a thorough licking. And such has been the case, similarly expressed, for some six hundred years. Thus John Gower wrote in his *Confessio Amantis* (1390), "O thou, which hast desesed [disseised] The Court of France be thi wrong, Now schalt thou singe an other song." Because the saying is so old we can assume that it arose from frequent use among wandering minstrels of the Middle Ages who, traveling from court to court, found it discreet to change the wording of the songs they sang to meet the boasts of each successive baron.

Indian giver

The most blameworthy charge that one child can level at another, for he (or she) so charged is two-faced, without honor, faithless. To be brief, the present that Billy-B may bring to Robbie's birthday party is one that Robbie may look at while the party is in progress,

 but Billy will demand its return when the party is over. That is to say, even back in colonial days an *Indian gift* referred "to the alleged custom among Indians," according to the *Handbook of American Indians* (1907) issued by the Smithsonian Institution, "of expecting an equivalent for a gift or otherwise its return." The same authority defines *Indian giver*—"A repentant giver." In my own youth, incidentally, although "Indian" was expected in for-

mal speech, the normal everyday speech of all boys and many adults was "Injun."

stool-pigeon

An informer or telltale; a decoy used by the police to trap a wrongdoer. The term is neither new nor recent. In the literal sense of a decoy pigeon it was in use by American hunters early in the nineteenth century. And fowlers also used the term "stool-crow," a similar decoy for crows. It is fairly certain that *stool* as used here was formerly written *stale*, which also meant a living bird used to attract others of its kind. Thus, for example, we have in Shakespeare's *The Tempest* (1611), IV, 1, "The trumpery in my house, goe bring it hither For *stale* to catch these theeues." And this in turn was a variation in the same period of *stall,* as in lines from the so-called Chester Whitsun Plays (*c.* 1500), "Send forth women of thie countrye, namely those that beautifull be, and to thie Enemyes lett them draw nye, as *stalles* to stand them before."

to pull up stakes

To move from a place; change one's location. This takes us back to colonial days in New England, to the time when a settler, dissatisfied for any cause with the parcel of land allotted to him, took up the boundary stakes and either returned to England or moved to another location of his own choosing. The earliest citation is to an English lawyer, Thomas Lechford, who, after a stay of two years in Boston, 1638 to 1640, wrote to a friend in England, "I am loth to hear of a stay [in New England], but am plucking up stakes, with as much speed as I may, if so be I may be so happy as to arrive in Ireland. . . ."

old (familiar) stamping ground

A place to which one is accustomed. Back in the Revolutionary period, and probably long earlier, a *stamping ground* was a place known to our American forebears where horses or other animals gathered in numbers. The step was short in a transference of the term to a place to which a man, woman, or child was accustomed. First to use it in a published work was H. R. Howard, compiler of

The History of Virgil A. Stewart (1836): "I made my way from Milledgeville to Williamson County, the old stamping-ground."

shiver my timbers

It is not at all likely that any self-respecting sailor would have ever thought of using or even dared to use such an ejaculation or oath as this, but, in 1834, the sailor and novelist, Frederick Marryat, finding the necessity for an oath, in *Jacob Faithful,* chapter XI, that would not offend the ears of the most puritanical reader invented this most innocuous expression: "I won't thrash you, Tom. Shiver my timbers if I do." John B. Opdyke, in *Mark My Words* (1949), page 584, says "the expression 'shiver my timbers' belongs to cricket, referring to scattering or strewing wickets for which *timbers* is a slang substitute." The statement is partly true, and would have been entirely true if he had said "was adopted by cricket," in which game it is now used.

to have (a person) where the hair is short; to get (a person) by the short hairs

Both expressions are in equal use and have identical meaning: to have or get a person at one's mercy; to have or get complete mastery over; or, more moderately, to have or get a decided advantage over. The metaphor appears to be of American origin; at least the earliest instance of literary use of these short hairs that has been found occurs in *Memoirs of the United States Secret Service* (1872), by George P. Burnham. Nowadays, thanks to modern hairdressing, the general assumption is that the reference is to the hair at the back of the head, just above the nape of the neck, now usually trimmed rather short among English-speaking people with whom the saying is familiar.

The saying undoubtedly antedates the time of its earliest literary use, however, and if one looks at portraits of, say, our presidents or other important figures of the Civil War period, men likely to be tonsorially correct, it is immediately evident that hair was not then cropped short. Accordingly, I think we should look elsewhere for the short hairs on which a grip would give one complete mastery over an antagonist. The pubic hairs could be considered, but, if such was the original allusion, the conflict that could have given rise to such a painful hold would necessarily have been one in which at least one of the contestants, such as an Indian, had a minimum of clothing. But it is also quite possible that the beard was intended, as in a fight between two white men. Our own Washington Irving, in *Knickerbocker's History of New York* (1809), wrote, "A gigantic question . . . which I must needs take by the beard and utterly subdue." It would certainly be a far easier hold to seize a man by the relatively short hairs of the beard than by the pubic hairs or the short hairs of the modern haircutter's art.

to put one's shoulder to the wheel

To assist with might and main; to labor vigorously in behalf of a cause, project, etc. In the physical sense one put one's shoulder to the wheel to aid his horse in pulling a cart or other vehicle out of the mud or over an obstacle. And when a horse required such aid, it was certain that vigorous effort was needed. No halfway measures are implied by the expression. Figurative usage dates back to the seventeenth century, but I have no doubt that the captive Israelites under the Pharaohs of ancient Egypt were often obliged to perform the task literally in the building of the pyramids.

to lose one's shirt

It means to lose everything one has, and, though this expression is fairly new, the concept of one's shirt being the last thing one possesses, next to his skin, is not exactly new. Chaucer conveyed that thought when, in "The Wyf of Bathes Tale," he wrote, "Who that holt [hold] him payd of his povert [poverty], I holde him riche, al [though] had he nought [not] a schert." It is the same idea which, for several centuries also, others have had in speaking of one who has "not a shirt to his back," or who had "given away the shirt off his back"—the last of his possessions, that is.

in seventh heaven

In a state of ineffable bliss or delight; having great pleasure. This, especially in Islamic beliefs, is the heaven of heavens, in its literal sense, the abode of God and the highest angels. A similar concept prevailed among the Jews in pre-Christian times, probably acquired from Babylonian beliefs. The concept calls for seven heavens, one lying above another, graded according to the degree of merit one has acquired on earth, or, in some beliefs, according to the successive steps taken by the soul after death.

to give short shrift to

To cut short; to make quick work of. The literal sense appears in Shakespeare's *The Tragedy of King Richard* III, Act IV, scene 4. Lord Hastings has just been sentenced to execution by the Duke of Gloucester, shortly to be declared Richard III, and is interrupted in his reveries by Ratcliff, ordered to oversee the execution, who says: "Dispatch, my lord; the duke would be at dinner: Make a short shrift; he longs to see your head." That is, though a condemned criminal was permitted time for confession or shrift, urgency might require that he be allowed no more than a few minutes for his shriving. Hence, thanks to the long list of crimes punishable by execution, this urgency was so common in the seventeenth century that "short shrift" became a synonym with "least possible delay."

spit-and-polish

Finical smartness or ornamentation; furbishment; trimness. But whereas in the early nineteenth century, and many years before, the British officer, naval and military, demanded such finicky smartness—as if by the application of much spittle and elbow grease with a polishing agent—by the latter half of that century many naval officers, at least, regarded it as a wasteful affectation, having no bearing on efficiency. The first to voice that disapproval—and, incidentally, to record the term—was Admiral Lord Charles Beresford. In his *Memoirs* (1914), telling of his first independent command in 1873, he said that though at the outset he had a large working party holystone the decks until they were "as clean as a hound's tooth," from that day onward "I set myself steadily against bright-work and spit-and-polish." And he added, "Under the spit-and-polish system no doubt the men take a pride in keeping the ship bright, but such a process involves perpetual extra bother and worry, which are quite unnecessary."

no great shakes

Nothing out of the ordinary in proficiency or achievement; no particular bargain; nothing of importance or consequence; nothing to write home about; no prize. Maybe, as suggested by the great *Oxford English Dictionary*, the ultimate source alluded to the shaking of dice, in which the turn is so often nothing more than mediocre. But the expression was such common slang in the begin-ning of the nineteenth century that Lord Broughton, writing of an incident that occurred in 1816 (in his *Recollections of a Long Life,* 1865), recalled that, to quote him, "W. said that a piece of sculp-ture there was '*nullae magnae quassationes*,' and the others laughed heartily." That is to say, the others present not only knew their Latin, but immediately recognized that, translated literally, it meant "no great shakes."

to hold the bag

To be left in the lurch, or in an awkward or ludicrous position not of one's own devising; to be made the scapegoat for faults com-mitted by others; to be the victim of a mean trick. As stated in *A Hog on Ice* this American expression was in use, and apparently

well understood, back in the time of George Washington, having been used in a comedy produced in 1787. But it did not occur to me, until reminded by several correspondents, that the expression un-doubtedly arose from the "snipe hunt" known to (and probably participated in by) my father some ninety years ago, often gleefully described to me, nor, in fact, that the boyhood hoax of central Ohio of his generation could have been brought from earlier settlements. How old the prank may be and when or where it may have originated, perhaps under another name, cannot be determined.

For the benefit of those unfamiliar with the game, this is the procedure: A group of boys, initiating a new boy in a community, invite him to join them some night on a "snipe hunt"—generally where snipe have never been seen. They take him far into the woods, wholly unfamiliar to him, armed with lanterns (or, nowadays, flashlights) and burlap bags. At a "likely" spot the new boy is handed one of the lanterns, is given a bag, and is instructed to keep the bag open, with the lantern above it, while the rest of the crowd go off into the brush to scare up the birds. The birds, he is told, seeing the light, will make for it and be caught in the bag. Of course, the rest of the crowd actually reassemble at some appointed spot and return hilariously to town and their own warm beds, leaving the neophyte, shivering and alone in a strange place,"holding the bag" for birds that will never appear.

Incidentally, among the Pennsylvania Dutch the hoax is known as *elbedritsch,* and there may be other names for it in other parts of the country.

to start from scratch

To begin any enterprise, investigation, search, or other activity from the very beginning, often with no precedent as a guide; to begin at the beginning; to take the first step. Actually the expression is derived from the sporting world, from a race in which *scratch* designates the line or mark that is to be the starting point. Hence, he who starts from scratch starts from nothing; he has no preliminary impetus beyond his own ability, genius, or determination to carry him through the race.

to go scotfree

To be free of penalty, or exempt from punishment or injury. Little Pete goes scotfree if mother thinks the costly new glass candlestick was knocked on the floor by the cat. But the expression and its extended meaning are very old. Back in the twelfth century a *scot* was a tax or forced contribution payable by the subjects of a municipality, later including the payment for one's share for entertainment in a tavern. Thus, as originally intended, a person who went scotfree was merely one who was free from the burden of paying a fine or tax, or, in a tavern, was under no obligation to pay a share of the score. As John de Trevisa wrote in *Bartholomeus* (1398): "After souper that is freely yeue [given] it is not honest to compell a man to pay his scot."

between wind and water

We go back to naval craft of the sixteenth century for this, and thence onward through the history of wooden vessels in warfare to recent times. The allusion is to that portion of the side of a ship which, especially in rough seas, is alternately above and below water, exposed both to wind and to water. A shot from a hostile gun striking such an area would be peculiarly hazardous. The historian George Bancroft made use of the expression in his account of the action between the United States and Tripoli in his *History of the United States* (1876). The frigate *Congress* was, as he described the action, "hulled twelve times, and hit seven times between wind and water." But the phrase has also been applied metaphorically to man for some three centuries, usually designating unexpected attack. The usage is illustrated in the sentence from Thomas Fuller's *The Church-History of England* (1655): "The good old man was shot between Wind and Water, and his consent was assaulted in a dangerous joincture of time to give any deniall."

not to care a straw

To be completely and utterly indifferent, or to regard as of no value whatever; not to care a tinker's dam. Stone floors were cold, back in the days when carpets or rugs had not yet come into general use, or when, as among the peasantry, none could afford or were permitted to own such luxuries. Hence, in the halls of the gentry, it was the custom in winter to spread straw rather thickly over the stone floors or, in the hovels of the common people, over the dirt floors. Accounts of the Lord High Treasurer of Scotland, in 1501, show a sum paid to one James Dog "to buy straw for the kingis chamer in Inverness." In summer, green rushes were used. Naturally, as Maria Leach points out in *The Soup Stone* (1954), such straw soon became trampled, broken, and filthy dirty. More straw scattered over the top might improve appearances briefly, but not for long. Scraps of food, bones tossed to the dogs, did nothing to improve sanitary conditions either. Obviously, straw placed to such use soon lost what little value it had ever had, becoming wholly worthless, as indicated by our common saying. But the trifling value of straw after the grain has been separated from it had also been recognized from earliest times.

gone where the woodbine twineth

When we were boys and either of us inquired as to the whereabouts of some article or person, mysteriously disappeared or vanished into thin air, my brother or I might answer, "Gone where the woodbine twineth and the whangdoodle mourneth for his firstborn." That is, somehow we picked up the saying in southern Ohio in the 1880's—both parts of the saying. Consequently, though I cannot produce proof, and though there is proof that the notorious stock manipulator, James Fisk, Jr., used the first clause in a statement quoted by New York newspapers in 1870 (when asked to account for a missing $50,000,000), and though the second clause appeared in an Illinois paper in 1858, I am confident that the whole expression was one of the highfalutin, boastful heroics of the rip-roaring breed of frontiersmen who salted their speech with all sorts of braggadocio in the early 1800's which we got in hand-me-down speech many years later. Jim Fisk, son of a peddler, could readily have picked it up in his youth, or later during his own peddling career.

to nourish a viper (or snake) in one's bosom

The saying takes us again to our old Greek friend, Aesop. The available translation tells this story under the title, "The Farmer and the Snake": "A Farmer found in the winter a Snake stiff and frozen with cold. He had compassion on it, and taking it up placed it in his bosom. The Snake on being thawed by the warmth quickly revived, when, resuming his natural instincts, he bit his benefactor, inflicting on him a mortal wound. The Farmer said with his latest breath, 'I am rightly served for pitying a scoundrel.' Moral: The greatest benefits will not bind the ungrateful."

as clean as a whistle

Robert Burns, in his poem, "Earnest Cry," used *toom* ("empty") rather than "clean"—"Paint Scotland greetan owre her thrissle; Her mutchkin stoup as toom's a whissle"—and other writers have had

· 111

the whistle clear, dry, pure, or other adjective. The basic intent, however, is to indicate that, for a sweet, pure sound from a whistle or reed, the tube must be clean and dry.

to go west

Although it has never been determined who, during World War I, was the first to speak of a fallen British soldier—and thereafter any member of the Allied military force who died in service—as having "gone west," the choice of the expression does not impress me as having been out of the ordinary. Any classical scholar could have expressed it thus. The association of death with the west goes back at least to Roman times. In fact our word *Occident*, by which we mean "west," the opposite of *Orient*, was derived from the Latin *occidere,* meaning "to kill" or "to die." That is, to the ancients, the sun "died" at the close of each day; the place where it died was *occidens*.

to say (or cry) "uncle"

To eat crow; throw in the towel or the sponge; cry quits; yield; submit. When I was a boy, one "hollered 'cavy' " when he was licked, but we would have been the most astonished boys in the world had anyone told us we were talking Latin. That is, "cavy," as I learned much later, is a corrupted contraction of *peccavi,* meaning, I have sinned, or, I am at fault, and this acknowledgment of guilt or fault was English usage from the sixteenth century onward. How it came into southern Ohio, I don't know. And our present American expression, though arising only in this century, may also have had Latin birth. At least, when the Roman lad was in trouble, he cried, *Patrue mi patruissime,* "Uncle, my best of uncles!"

on velvet

Although the *Wardrobe Accounts of Edward II* state that that British sovereign (1307–27) had "1 couerchief de veluett" (kerchief of velvet), this material was still so rare and costly through the next two or three hundred years, so generally unfamiliar, as not to acquire any figurative application. Thus it was only about two centuries ago that our present common expression began to indicate prosperity, a condition of ease or comfort. It was sufficiently well known, that is, to justify its use by Edmund Burke when, as Premier, in 1769, he stated in his notable *Observations on a Pamphlet on the Present State of the Nation* that not like the author of that pamphlet "who is always on velvet, he is aware of some difficulties."

tune the old cow died of

Any tune with which one has become thoroughly fed up, or the instrument upon which a tune is played ad nauseam, or the tedious or tiresome manner in which a tune is played. Some of the theme compositions of modern radio and television I would class as "tunes

the old cow died of." And the bagpipe and certain other so-called musical instruments could be consigned to the same category—in my humble opinion. In fact, concerning the bagpipe, I thought for a while I had the real reason for the death of the old cow. I figured that, in ancient times at least, the udder of the cow might have been used as the bag of the pipe and the various appendages might have been utilized for air intake, pipes, and drone respectively. The theory was good, but, alas, no history of bagpipe construction bears it out. All I can do, therefore, is to play follow the leader and report the childish yarn of the anonymous "old ballad" which would cause the death of any cow, old or young:

> There was an old man, and he had an old cow,
>   But he had no fodder to give her,
> So he took up his fiddle, and played her a tune;
>   "Consider, good cow, consider,
> This isn't the time for the grass to grow,
>   Consider, good cow, consider."

to wash one's dirty linen in public

All we did, about a century ago, was to reverse the French proverb, *il faut laver son linge sale en famille,* "one should wash one's dirty linen in private." The French idea, that is, is that family quarrels or matters that concern members of the family should be kept within the four walls of the home. Anthony Trollope seems to have heard the French saying, or was at least the first to give us the English equivalent. This was in *The Last Chronicle of Barset* (1867): "I do not like to trouble you with my private affairs;—there is nothing, I think, so bad as washing one's dirty linen in public."

to go to the wall

Though now it is usually a business house that, under insurmountable financial difficulties, "goes to the wall," it was—back in the sixteenth century—the adversary in a conflict that, forced to yield ground, went to the wall. The allusion is to the desperate straits of a wayfarer when set upon by ruffians in an unlighted street of former years. By giving ground and getting his back to the wall he was better able to defend himself by poniard or sword. From the same situation, by no means uncommon in the Middle Ages and later, came our expression, "to be driven (or pushed) to the wall," which we now use in a similar sense, to be forced to one's last resource.

to throw cold water

It's all a matter of habitual practice or personal taste. That is, if one is not accustomed to a cold shower, a sudden dash of cold water on one's naked body may be quite a shock. The very notion, a hundred and fifty years ago, gave one the jitters, or at least "dampened" one's ardor. Thus the deliberate throwing of cold water was taken to be an unfriendly act. And, in figurative usage, the thrower then became one who discouraged a plan or project or who was cool toward it.

to meet one's Waterloo

To get one's come-uppance; to meet defeat. Any reader of the life of Napoleon will recognize the source and the significance of the phrase. After the defeat of the "little Corsican" by the Allies in 1814 and his brief imprisonment on Elba, from which he escaped in February of 1815, Napoleon again took the field against his enemies in June. Nominally he had an army of 500,000 men, but he actually mustered only 198,000. Opposed to him were the English, Dutch, Belgian, Prussian, and Austrian forces, numbering about 215,000 men—121,000 under Blucher and about 94,000 under Wellington. The two adversaries met near the little village of Waterloo, Belgium, some twelve miles south of Brussels. Despite a more advantageous position at the beginning of the battle on the morning of June 18, the French army was overwhelmingly defeated, its retreat ending in a rout. Napoleon was again forced to abdicate and was then imprisoned on the island of St. Helena until his death in 1821.

to beat (or belt) the living daylights out of one

To beat severely; flog unmercifully; lick the stuffing or tar out of one, or many other synonyms for thrash, punish, chastise. All these indicate severe punishment that is to be administered to a foe or even to a son, but none is so drastic as the original and less verbose threat. That is, back in the late eighteenth century or, most probably earlier, one threatened "to let daylight into" someone, usually a foe. This was, or was to be, accomplished by means of an opening made into his system by a dagger or sword or other sharp-pointed instrument or, in later times, by a bullet. But such actual punishment bore attendant risk of reprisal by law, so the threats became more moderate. One was less likely to swing for merely thrashing a person, and, certainly, "living daylights" could not be interpreted as a threat of death. The suspicion is that the modified phrase is of American origin, dating back perhaps seventy-five years.

like a bump on a log

Like a Stoughton bottle; stolid; unemotional; stupidly dumb. Usually any such dumb bunny is said to sit or stand like a bump on a log, meaning just to sit or stand in vacuous silence. The metaphor is American and may have referred originally to the stolid protuberance found on almost any log, or it may have been suggested as a comparison of the discomfort from sitting on a bumpy log with the discomfort of association with a superbly dumb companion. Undoubtedly the description was used long before her time, but it seems to have appeared first in Kate Douglas Wiggins' *The Bird's*

Christmas Carol (1899): "Ye ain't goin' to set there like a bump on a log 'thout sayin' a word to pay for yer vittles, air ye?"

double-cross

Betrayal; treachery; deception by double-dealing; or, as a verb, to bamboozle; to take one to the cleaners. Like any other slang expression this may have been current for many years before it received recognition on the printed page. Its formation, however, was a natural one: the adjective *double* in the sense, "characterized by duplicity; false," and the noun *cross* in its slang sense, "dishonesty; fraudulence." The first record we have is in the 1874 edition of John Hotten's *Dictionary of Modern Slang, Cant, and Vulgar Words,* with the definition—still in vogue in prize fights and some other sports—"A cross in which a man who has engaged to lose breaks his engagement, and 'goes straight' at the last moment."

to get one's come-uppance

To receive the fate one has merited; to get what is coming to one in the way of chastisement or rebuke. Though "come-uppance," in the sense here used, is said to be dialectal English, I think it is American, perhaps a modification of English usage, however. Our cousins spoke of one's "come-uppings," rather than "come-uppance," and the latter has been our usage since the Civil War at least. The phrase was in use long before his time, but William Dean Howells gave it the stamp of literary approval when, in *Silas Lapham* (1884), he wrote: "Rogers is a rascal . . . But I guess he'll find he's got his come-uppance."

trade last (or T. L.)

A quoted compliment offered by one who heard it in exchange for a compliment; reciprocal praise; adulatory tit-for-tat. Although a contributor to *American Speech* (October–December, 1948) tells of a friend of seventy-odd who "has known *trade last* in Kansas as far back as she can remember," the expression was sheer Greek to me when, coming from Ohio, I first heard it on Staten Island, New York, in the very early 1890's. In either case, however, that would indicate that it was used as early as the 1880's. But where it originated and under what circumstance cannot be guessed. "Last," in the expression, means that the speaker will not submit his tidbit of praise until the prospective recipient has first come across with a compliment, but why the adjective follows the noun is another mystery. The abbreviation to *T. L.* was introduced some forty years ago, probably a collegiate coinage which speedily became so popular that many young people are unfamiliar with the words so abbreviated.

to blow one's own horn

To advertise oneself; boast of one's own abilities; brag. In England, the same self-advertising is done by "blowing one's own trumpet," and there is every reason to assume that this saying, or variants thereof, was the source of the  American phrase. Fleming, in *A Panoplie of Epistles* (1576), "sounded" the trumpet of his own "merites," and writers of the eighteenth century "blew" their trumpets. The earliest American usage, according to Bartlett's *Dictionary of Americanisms* (1877), was "blowin' his bazoo," which was defined, "gasconade; braggadocio"—terms meaning boastful talk. At some time since that date—and on a guess I'd say about seventy-five years ago—the slang term "bazoo" began to drop out of favor and "horn" became the accepted substitute.

to make the air blue

Just why a vigorous and plentiful use of cuss words is supposed by us figuratively to affect the color of the atmosphere, especially to give it a blue tone, is a matter of guesswork. The history of our language does not show how the concept arose. The association of "blue" with evil is not altogether recent, however. Back in 1742 Edward Young in *Night Thoughts on Life, Death and Immortality,* wrote, "Riot, pride, perfidy, blue vapours breathe," in which he referred to "blue" as the color of plagues. And baleful demons were described as "blue devils" more than a hundred years earlier when, in 1616, these lines appeared in *The Times' Whistle*:

> Alston, whose life hath been accounted evill,
> And therefore calde by many the blew devill.

Joseph P. Roppolo, of the Department of English, Tulane University, discussing the use of "blue" in the sense, indecent, obscene, suggests the possibility of the following explanation, in *American Speech*, Vol. XXVIII, No. 1:

Early in its history, *blue* acquired symbolic meanings which are diametrically opposed. As the color of the clear sky and of the sea (both good), it came to be the symbol of purity, of fidelity, of staunchness, and of faith, and, by symbolic extension, it was chosen as one of the colors of the Virgin. Perhaps simultaneously (since both extremes involve morality and seem to be connected with the Christian religion), a flame which burned blue came to be associated with the flames of burning brimstone and therefore of hell; such a flame, quite logically, was regarded by the superstitious as an omen of death or other evil or was believed to indicate the presence of ghosts or evil spirits or of the devil himself. From these beliefs, it seems probable, developed *blue-blazes*, meaning hell, and such statements as "he talked blue" and "he made the air blue," meaning, respectively, "He talked obscenely" and "He cursed and swore": cursing or sinful talk would evoke evil spirits or the devil, whose sulphurous presence would cause flames to burn blue. Such talk, again logically, although this is admittedly conjecture, would become *blue talk*, and an oath or a curse a *blue word*.

cash on the barrelhead

Immediate payment; spot cash; payment on the nail. There is no doubt in my mind that the original scene here was the makeshift bar of the American frontier a century or more ago. The barrel itself, under improvised conditions, served as both container and counter, or, when empty, as counter only. But the wise bartender trusted none of his customers and extended no credit. Nor did he dare turn to serve another lest the first vamoose, and he unable to give chase. The expression dates back many years, but, regrettably, none but recent uses have been found. Its modern equivalent is the weak "cash on the counter."

to talk a blue streak

To talk rapidly and, usually, interminably. We seem to have made this up from two or more other American expressions, all referring to lightning. As long ago as 1830, for instance, mail coaches, though drawn by horses, moved with such rapidity as to leave a "blue streak" behind them. And if one "made a streak for home," or any other designation, he was in such a hurry to get there that, figuratively, he ran like lightning. Or it could be that we have partly taken a German expression, *das Blaue vom Himmel schwatzen,* to chatter the blue from the skies. The British equivalent is "to talk off a donkey's hind legs," which with us is "to talk one's arm off," in modern slang.

the real McCoy

In *A Hog on Ice* I attributed this expression to a prize fighter of the late nineties who traveled under the ring-name of "Kid McCoy." Another fighter of lesser skill, my story went, somewhat the worse for drink and unaware that McCoy was within hearing distance, declared in a barroom that he could lick any of the McCoys, any time and any place. When he picked himself up from the sawdust, after "The Kid" had delivered a haymaker, he amended his remarks by saying that he had meant any of the fighters who had adopted the popular name, "any but the real McCoy."

Although that version has earmarks of veracity, or at least of near veracity, other widely different explanations of the origin of the phrase have been made. Thus, in 1946 a writer in the New Orleans *Picayune,* as quoted in *A Dictionary of Americanisms* (1951), says, "The term originally was applied to heroin brought in from the island of Macao off the coast of China. . . . It was not cut. Dope addicts found out the stuff from Macao was the real Macao." The editor of that dictionary, however, Mitford M. Mathews, does not now accept that explanation, nor do I. Instead, according to his statement in *American Speech,* May, 1953, he regards with favor the solution proposed by Eric Partridge in *From Sanskrit to Brazil,* (1952). The corresponding British phrase, *the real Mackay,* Partridge says, dates from the 1880's and was originally Scottish, applied first to men of excellent quality and then to first-rate things, especially whiskey. The latter, namely the product of A. & M. MacKay of Glasgow, was exported to America where, Partridge believes, Scottish settlers in Canada and the United States were plentiful enough to "keep both the whisky and the phrase very much alive," though the phrase was later "transformed to *the real McCoy,* first under the impact of the hero worship that, in the late 1890's accrued to boxer Kid McCoy and then under that which, in the early 1920's, accrued, at least in New York State, to bootlegger Bill McCoy." I quote this theory for what it is worth, though it seems far-fetched to me. It is a fact, nevertheless, that the term *McCoy,* in slang usage, did refer to whisky of good quality back in 1908, a date earlier than any literary evidence of the usage of the entire phrase.

all my eye (and Betty Martin)

All humbug; sham; stuff and nonsense; apparent but not real; imaginary. The age, even of the first part of this expression, is unknown. Grose, in *A Classical Dictionary of the Vulgar Tongue* (1785), was the first to give it mention, but it is likely that "all in my eye"—that is, all imaginary—was an earlier phrase for the same thing. The second part, "and Betty Martin," has been the subject of much speculation. In commenting on the expression in *The Doctor* (1837), Robert Southey says, "Who was Betty Martin, and wherefore should she be so often mentioned in connection with my precious eye or yours?"

But Grose did not make proper nouns of the words. His listing of the phrase reads: "That's my eye betty martin." That gave some grounds for the explanation that appeared in some of the later editions of the apocryphal book, *Joe Miller's Jests.* Therein it was said that a sailor, attracted by the music, wandered into a Catholic church. The Latin words puzzled him. But finally a phrase caught his ear, *Ah mihi, beate Martin,* (Ah! grant me, blessed St. Martin), but to a comrade he later confessed that this he had understood to be, "All my eye and Betty Martin." This explanation might pass muster, except for the fact, alas, that no such Latin prayer is to be found in the formulary of the Catholic Church.

off one's base

This has a literal meaning in baseball, referring to a position taken by a runner away from the bag or base he has occupied, but in the slang sense it has nothing to do with baseball. Here *base* pertains to that which supports a person, and the expression thus  means mentally unbalanced; crazy; off one's rocker or bean; screwy. One of the earliest to use the expression in print was George W. Peck, author of *Sunshine* (1882) and *Peck's Bad Boy and His Pa* (1883). In Chapter II of the latter: ". . . the boy has been for the three weeks trying to think of some innocent joke to play on his father. The old man is getting a little near sighted, and his teeth are not as good as they used to be, but the old man will not admit it . . . and he would bet a hundred dollars that he could see as far as ever. The boy knew the failing, and made up his mind to demonstrate to the old man that he was rapidly getting off his base." The means taken, incidentally, was that the bad boy cut up some small rubber hose and, with the connivance of the "hired girl," mixed it into his pa's serving of macaroni. The mischief was eventually discovered—and the boy had another session in the woodshed.

with a high hand

Overbearing in manner; arrogantly. In the Bible—Numbers xxxiii, 3—the chronicler used the expression in the sense of "triumphantly," in the description of the departure of the Israelites from Egyptian bondage: "And they departed from Rameses in the first month, on the fifteenth day of the first month; on the morrow after the passover the children of Israel went out with an high hand in the sight of all the Egyptians." In fact, it was through Wyclif's translation of the Bible in 1382 that we have the metaphor—"Therfor thei goon forth . . . in an hig hoond."

to turn the heat on

Of course we "turn the heat on," in this modern age, when we adjust the thermostat to a higher thermometer reading, and thus start up the oil-burning or gas-fired furnace or the electric heater. But in current slang, the "heat" is of a different nature. At first, it would seem, it was that of the electric chair, called in criminal jargon the "hot seat." But then, approximately the time of the First World War, it became a slang substitute for the accepted colloquialism of three centuries standing, "to make it hot for," that is, to make one extremely uncomfortable, as by the grilling of a district attorney. More recently, the "heat" has been extended to include search for a person suspected of crime, and it may be even a master criminal who "turns on the heat" when grilling a subordinate.

to keep one's pecker up

To maintain one's courage or resolution; not to get down in the mouth; to keep a stiff upper lip. In fact, we might say that "lip" and "pecker" are two terms for the same thing, as the lip corresponds with the beak or pecker of a bird. The expression dates to about the middle of the nineteenth century.

to harp on one string

To repeat one thing endlessly; to dwell upon one theme at great length; to bore one to extinction with one bit of advice or caution or the like; to tell the same tale over and over again. The allusion is, of course, obvious. If a harpist were to play her instrument upon one note, the monotony would probably drive her nuts, if some unwilling listener had not already killed her. Although the harp was known in Biblical times, the English saying is first recorded in the early sixteenth century.

to split hairs

To quibble; to make fine distinctions; to cavil or become captious over trifles. Thanks to the great degree of refinement in modern equipment, a hair may be split or divided lengthwise into numerous fine filaments. In fact, not long since, we were told of a drill so fine that a series of minute holes could be bored transversely across a hair. But in the seventeenth, the eighteenth, and even the nineteenth century it was still considered no more possible to split a hair than for a camel to pass through the eye of a needle. Hence, anyone arguing over trifles or quibbling about inconsequential matters was likened to anyone who would attempt to split a hair.

in hot water

In trouble; in a pretty kettle of fish; in a pretty how-de-do; behind the 8-ball; on the spot; up Salt Creek; domestically, in the dog house. When one considers that, during the Dark Ages especially, one of the favorite tests of guilt or innocence of a crime called for the dipping of the hand or arm in boiling water and picking up a stone or ring, it might be reasonable to suppose that our present expression owes its origin to that ordeal. But, no. Though the phrase undoubtedly arose from the extreme discomfort produced by scalding water, the colloquial sense so familiar to all began merely as eighteenth-century slang.

by the great horn spoon

A mild oath, about as innocuous as "by the beard of the prophet," not as strong as "great jumping Jehoshaphat." Delvers into our language have been trying to figure out just what a "great horn spoon" was. So far, the search has been unsuccessful. Apparently it first occurred in a song printed in 1842 in which these lines occur: "He vow'd by the great horn spoon. . . . He'd give them a licking, and that pretty soon." I have tried to find a copy of that song in order to determine the allusions, but have not yet discovered one.

Of course, horn spoons—spoons shaped from the curved horns of cattle—were in common use for many centuries before the comparatively recent introduction of cheap, durable metals. But why a horn spoon should suddenly become "great" is still conjectural.

A correspondent, Francis W. Palmer, to the October–December, 1949, issue of *American Speech,* tries to connect the great horn with the American "bighorn," the Rocky Mountain sheep, which were called *gros cornes,* "great horns," by early French explorers. And he finds that Francis Parkman, in *The California and Oregon Trail* (1849), says the Indians made "ladles with long handles, capable of holding more than a quart, cut from such horns." But to me it does not seem likely that the writer of the song mentioned above could have known that fact in 1842.

to keep one's eye on the ball

To be closely attentive; to be alert, alive and kicking, on one's toes; to sit up and take notice. This has been popular American speech in a figurative sense for at least fifty years. In source, although applicable to any sport in which a ball is kept in motion—tennis, golf, billiards, bowls, polo—it was probably the game of football from which it was derived, from the urgent instructions of college coaches.

call off the dogs

Cease some objectionable line of conduct, procedure, conversation, inquiry, or the like; break off an unprofitable or disagreeable course. The analogy is that of the chase, in which dogs following a wrong scent are called off.

to hoe one's own row

To make one's own way; to be independent, beholden to no one; to paddle one's own canoe, peddle one's own papers, blow one's own nose. This was farm lingo, and is still applicable in a literal sense on any farm on which most labor is performed without benefit of machinery. Figurative application apparently dates to a time shortly after the death of William Henry Harrison (April 4, 1841), a month after inauguration, when John Tyler succeeded him as president. Tyler, a former Democrat, had broken with his party and was elected with Harrison on the belief that he had fully adopted Whig principles. But within a few months it became evident that such was not the case. With the exception of Daniel Webster, Secretary of State, the entire cabinet resigned (September, 1841). This led a writer in *The Knickerbocker*, a New York monthly, to say, "Our American pretender must, to adopt an agricultural phrase, 'hoe his own row,' . . . without the aid of protectors or dependents."

a sop to Cerberus

Cerberus, in classical mythology, was the three-headed dog that guarded the entrance to Hades, permitting the dead to enter, but preventing their shades from leaving. Sometimes those who entered were greeted in friendly manner by the several heads, but others might be met by fierce and angry snarls. Accordingly, friends placed in the hands of those who died honey cakes to be fed to Cerberus, thus to permit them a friendly entrance, as described in Bishop Gavin Douglas's translation of the *Aeneid* (1513), VI, vi, 69:

. . . Cerberus, the hiduus hund, that regioun
Fordynnys, barkand with thre mowthis ſowm,
Onmeſurabill in his cave quher he lay
Richt our for gane thame in the hie way:
Quhom till the prophete, behaldand quhou in hy
Hys nekkis wolx of eddyrris all gryſly
A ſop, ſtepyt intill hunny als faſt,
And of enchant it cornys maid, gan caſt.

Hence, figuratively, "a sop to Cerberus" is any gift or compliment or the like that may placate an opponent, allay suspicion, or distract vigilance.

a long (or hard) row to hoe

A difficult or tedious task to perform; a dreary prospect to face. An American expression of obvious source, and there are few tasks more dispiriting to face than to start hoeing weeds from a long, long row of beans, say, or to hill a row of corn that seems to stretch ahead interminably. First to use the figurative sense in print was David Crockett, in his book with the lengthy title, *An Account of Col. Crockett's Tour to the North and Down East, in the Year of the Lord One Thousand Eight Hundred and Thirty-four* (1835): "I never opposed Andrew Jackson for the sake of popularity. I knew it was a hard row to hoe, but I stood up to the rack."

mad as a wet hen

Very, very vexed. Though, unlike a duck, a hen does not deliberately seek water in a pond and is not disposed to leave a dry shelter in search of food in the rain, this metaphor has never made good sense to me. My sons and daughters have, at various times, sought small fortunes from chickens (with much of the care devolving upon me), but I have never seen a hen becoming particularly perturbed from getting wet. If she has a brood of chicks, she will cluck them under the shelter of her wings during a shower, but she certainly doesn't stamp her feet and rave noisily, no matter how wet she herself becomes. Yet many a man, woman, and child, with far lesser cause, is said to become "mad as a wet hen." Be that as it may, whether sensible or not, the expression has been good American since at least 1823, as determined by a correspondent in *American Speech*, Vol. XXI: "Every body that was not ax'd was mad as a wet hen."

as scarce as (or scarcer than) hen's teeth

No one has ever yet found teeth in a hen, nor is likely to; so this is just another example (American) of exaggerated statement not intended to be taken literally, to impress the listener with the fact that the item under discussion, whatever it may be, does not exist, rarely occurs, or is rarely to be found. Thus one might say, "Elephants in Greenland are scarcer than hen's teeth," meaning that elephants are not to be found in Greenland. Just when this hyperbole first appeared has not yet been determined. *The Dictionary of Americanisms* reports its use by "Edmund Kirke," pen name of James R. Gilmore, in *My Southern Friends* (1862). But because this metaphor is thoroughly familiar in all parts of the country, there's good reason to believe that it may actually have had word-of-mouth use from colonial days.

from hell to breakfast

I have little doubt that the original expression was "hell-bent for breakfast," cowboy slang of the past thirty or forty years, typifying the rush from bunkhouse to cookshack at the clang of the breakfast gong—automobile-tire rim or triangle. In fact, some writers still have their characters say, "hell for breakfast," though the heading I have used is, I think, more common. But whereas "hell for breakfast" signifies in a hell of a hurry, "from hell to breakfast," though sometimes used with the same sense, usually connotes nothing more than "from Dan to Beersheba"; that is, a lot of territory.

cross one's heart

The most binding oath of childhood; solemn assurance of truthfulness, usually accompanied by motions of the right hand forming a cross over the general vicinity of the testator's heart. Probably the gesture and its binding nature were originally based upon the familiar Catholic sign of the cross. In my own Protestant childhood in Ohio, and my wife says the same was the case in Massachusetts, the oath was often accompanied by the irreverent doggerel: "Cross my heart and hope to die, And hope the cat'll spit in your eye."

old hat

Old stuff; information, experience, condition, or the like that is familiar. A gutter interpretation of the origin, based on the pun, "frequently felt," does not strike me as remotely plausible. In my opinion the familiarity that is implied is rather that of long usage, something to which one is as accustomed as he is to a hat so long worn as to fit the head snugly. The metaphor is comparatively recent, and is rarely heard in the United States.

duck soup

Extremely easy; easy as rolling off a log; hence, a cinch. American slang of some twenty-five years' standing. Probably derived from "a sitting duck," namely one resting on the water, thus easily shot by a hunter; hence, figuratively, an easy mark, any person who lays himself wide open to ridicule or any form of attack. Thus, to some persons, the solution of a cross-word puzzle or the putting together of a jigsaw puzzle is duck soup.

to ride the gravy train

To acquire wealth; become prosperous; live on Easy Street; have a profitable business or an easy or well-paid position. Probably the expression actually arose in railroading lingo, in which a *gravy run* or a *gravy train* meant an easy run with good pay for the train crew, for *gravy* in popular speech, has long meant money easily earned or obtained. Though the earliest quotation in which *gravy train* appears is in Benjamin A. Botkin's *Lay My Burden Down* (1945)—"They is on the gravy train and don't know it, but they is headed straight for 'struction and perdition"—even the full phrase, "to ride the gravy train," was undoubtedly in use ten or twenty years earlier than that date, because it appears in all the above senses in *The American Thesaurus of Slang* which was published in 1942 and was under compilation during the preceding ten years or so.

in the doghouse

In a predicament; in a pickle; in a pretty how-de-do; in disgrace. This American slang of the early twentieth century came into being through analogy. Anyone who was considered, usually by a man's wife, to be "going to the dogs" was, in theory at least, thought to  be fit to associate only with the family dog, especially for slumber; hence, figuratively, consigned to the dog kennel. The notion became enlarged. In due course the husband began to realize that any time he was going to have domestic difficulty, especially in explaining an action, he would again be out of favor and again be relegated to the doghouse.

getting down to grass-roots

This is something that politicians or office-seekers repeatedly do, or do in their speechifying preceding an election. Grass-roots, apparently, are rediscovered perennially at those times. Actually, this homely American phrase means nothing more than getting down to the underlying principles or basic facts of a matter, and may be appropriately used at any time. Popularity preceding an election indicates that it is then that politicians strive to convince their hearers that they know all basic facts troubling the nation.

Mencken, in *Supplement One: The American Language* (1945) says in a footnote: "The late Dr. Frank H. Vizetelly told me in 1935 that he had been informed that *grass-roots,* in the verb-phrase, *to get down to grass-roots,* was in use in Ohio *c.* 1885, but he could never track down the printed record of it, and neither could I." Well, I guess I'm the culprit. The phrase has been familiar to me, through my father's use of it, ever since I was still wearing skirts in my Ohio infancy, and it is probable that, questioned by my then boss, "Dr. Viz," I said that it had been used in Ohio for at least fifty years—and I still think I was right.

to ring a bell

To start a train of recollection; to strike a familiar chord; also, to appeal to one, to strike one's fancy. Partridge, in *A Dictionary of Slang,* says that this is from "the bell that rings when, at a shooting-gallery, a marksman hits the bull's-eye." I don't agree with that. In my opinion, this expression, with its indefinite article, is of nostalgic birth, relating rather to memories or responses evoked by the church bell or the school bell. Had he specified the American expression, "to ring the bell," always with the definite article, I could agree. That expression indicates success in one form or another; as, in a commercial transaction, to make a sale or obtain an order for goods; in law, to win a case; in games, to make a high score; in sports, to win; on the turf, to finish first; in gambling, to win a bet; in one's studies, to pass an examination. These all spring from target shooting.

come (or in spite of) hell or high water

Let the consequences be whatever they may, however ill. I'd say that this is considerably older than the date—1915—shown for it in *A Dictionary of Americanisms.* In fact, I heard it commonly employed in Colorado and Wyoming some years earlier, and it is the sort of expression that one would expect to find studded through Bret Harte's Western stories. And, though the dictionaries describe "high water" as either being about the same thing as ordinary highest tide or ordinary highest flow of a stream, I'd translate the "high water" of this saying as referring specifically to the flash floods of water that roll down a canyon after a heavy storm above, sweeping everything before it. Certainly that's the kind of destructive force worthy of comparison with "hell."

sound (or all right) on the goose

Back in 1854 Congress, admitting Kansas and Nebraska as territories, weakly made the slave question a matter of local option. But abolitionists among the new settlers were at first in the minority. "How are you on the goose?" became a customary question put to any newcomer in a community, especially in Kansas. It was never clear just how the term "goose" became involved in the question of slavery, but if the answer was "All sound (or all right) on the goose," the newcomer was recognized to be in favor of slavery and was usually welcomed to the community. But if the answer was "I'm a free-stater," one who wanted Kansas to become a free state, he was likely to be looked upon with disfavor or threatened or told to move on. Though Kansas eventually entered the Union as a free state, this particular "goose" brought about not only the John Brown rebellion, but also the birth of the Republican Party, replacing the Whig Party, and ultimately led to the disastrous War between the States.

to fish or cut bait

To make a choice; specifically, to be obliged to take a definite stand, as upon a political issue. Just how this personal decision, admitting of no argument, wandered from matters piscatorial to matters political is one of the many questions which contribute interest to the life of a lexicographer, questions that often remain unanswered forever.

Cutting bait is one of the essential duties on board a deep-sea fishing vessel. Live fish, carried for the purpose, are cut into chunks which are then dropped overboard in quantity to attract the quarry when the vessel has reached a favorable location. The duty is onerous, but is assigned summarily to a member of the crew who, in the opinion of the captain, has merited it.

Though this American expression had undoubtedly long been part of the common argot of fisher folk, it suddenly appeared with political significance in the halls of Congress back in 1876, and from the mouth of a representative, not of a salt-water state, but of the inland state of Illinois, Joseph Gurney Cannon, then known as "the Hayseed Member from Illinois"—years later affectionately termed "Uncle Joe." On August 5th of that year in a discussion of a monetary bill, Cannon pointed out that the bill was open to amendment, and then declared: "I will offer what is known as the Kelley silver bill as an additional section to the bill." Then according to the *Congressional Record,* he added:

Now I want you gentlemen on the other side of the House to "fish or cut bait." This is the chance and the only chance you will have under the rules this session by which a bill can be passed by a majority vote, making the silver dollar a legal tender for all debts, public and private. Gentlemen of the other side [the Democratic side], do something positive for once during this session . . .

ivory tower

When Charles-Augustin Sainte-Beuve, French literary critic of the early nineteenth century, coined this term he thought of it as applicable to the aerie of a poet, a place where he could retire from the world, a retreat. The term occurs in his own poem, *Pensées d'Août* (*Thoughts of August*), written in October, 1837, and dedicated to François Villemain. The third stanza, in which Victor Hugo and Alfred de Vigny, both poets, are mentioned, runs in part—

> Hugo, dur partisan
> . . . combattit sous l'armure,
> Et tint haut sa bannière ou milieu du murmure:
> Il la maintient encore; et Vigny, plus secret,
> Comme en sa tour d'ivoire, avant midi, rentrait.

> [Hugo, strong partisan
> . . . fought in armor,
> And held high his banner in the midst of the tumult;
> He still holds it; and Vigny, more discreet,
> As if in his tower of ivory, retired before noon.]

Nevertheless, although Saint-Beuve may be credited as the originator of the thought, its intent is more pertinently expressed

by Jules de Gaultier in *La Guerre et les Destinées de l'Art,* as given
also in the Christopher Morley edition of *Bartlett's Familiar Quotations* (1948):

The poet, retired in his Tower of Ivory, isolated, according to his
desire, from the world of man, resembles, whether he wishes or not,
another solitary figure, the watcher enclosed for months at a time in a
lighthouse at the head of a cliff.

Though long held by the poets, the "ivory tower" has been in-
vaded by others in recent years. It is still aloof from the common
run and is still a sanctum, but, whether secluded or not, it is now a
remote observation post that is open to philosophers, college professors, various writers, an occasional editor, and others who may,
as from a place of vantage, watch the world go by.

a whipping boy

One upon whom is inflicted punishment for the faults or wrongs
of another; a scapegoat. Under the belief that the body of a young
royal prince was as sacred as that of the king, his father, and that,
accordingly, no governess nor tutor should chastise him, a custom
was introduced into England in the early seventeenth century to
transfer any punishment merited by a princeling to the body of another. The first to benefit was the son of James I, the young prince
who later became Charles I. The lad William Murray was appointed
to be his playmate and fellow pupil, and to receive all punishment
deserved by either of the two lads, to be the "whipping boy" of the
prince and be flogged for all the faults of either. The custom died
out as the royal household became more democratic, but the allusion has remained.

to suck the hind teat

In my youth, it was "tit" rather than "teat," of course, but there
was then long established American usage for that. The allusion
was to the supposition long existing among the breeders of domestic
animals that the rearmost nipple of an udder supplied less nourish-
ment to a calf, colt, piglet, or lamb than any of the others; hence,
that any of a litter forced by its brothers and sisters to draw from

that poor source of supply was bound to be a weakling. Accordingly, the expression as I have always known it has meant to lose out, to get the short end of the stick, to have the worst of a deal. However, in the Ozarks, according to E. H. Criswell, in *American Speech,* December, 1953, a meaning given to the phrase in that region is "to be always late or behind," though he offers no conjectural explanation. Typical American prudery affords no example of literary use.

over a barrel

When you have one "over a barrel" or put him over one you have him at your mercy, on the spot; you have him under your

thumb—hook, line, and sinker. I surmise that the literal expression was an act of mercy, arising from the use of a barrel, until better means of resuscitation were developed, in the attempt to bring a drowned person back to life. In that method the person taken from the water was placed face down over the curving surface of a barrel, which was then gently rolled. Needless to add, the one so placed was at the mercy of the attendant.

to throw in the sponge (or towel)

To say uncle; to holler quits; to admit defeat; to surrender, submit, or yield. In today's pugilistic encounters one is more likely to hear that the manager of one contestant throws in a towel, rather than a sponge, but the original occasion for the expression, which still stands in a non-physical sense, is explained in *The Slang Dictionary.* Though first published in 1860, the 1874 edition in my possession reads: " 'To throw up the sponge,' to submit, to give over the struggle—from the practice of throwing up the sponge used to cleanse a combatant's face at a prize-fight, as a signal that the side on which that particular sponge has been used has had enough—that the sponge is no longer required."

to crack the whip

To be in control; to have absolute dominance; to have under one's thumb; to rule the roost. The Florida "cracker," nowadays, tries to persuade himself and others that this nickname originated, not, as was actually the case, because his antecedents were notorious braggarts—i.e., cracked tall tales—but, as was not the case, because they were drovers, who cracked the whip over cattle or teams of oxen or mules.

Our present expression, however, did originate from the skill of drovers or teamsters in handling the vicious bullwhacker whip of, especially, the nineteenth century. Before the days of the railroad, or to areas unreached by them, large wheeled wagons drawn by two, four, six or more pairs of horses, mules, or oxen carted freight over mountains and plains to ever-extending Western frontiers. The whip or bullwhacker of the driver, though short-handled, carried a long heavy thong which, properly wielded, could be snapped through the air to sound like a shot from a gun. Some drivers became so expert as, reputedly, to be able to kill a horsefly from the flanks of the leading horse without disturbing a hair of the animal, or to flick a piece of the hide from a lagging "critter." All these were the ones who, originally, "cracked the whip."

to jump Jim Crow

To dance with a peculiar limping step. Although, according to the *Negro Year Book* for 1925–26, the name "Jim Crow" was that of a Negro born in Richmond about 1800, later emancipated and, in England, acquiring "quite a fortune," it is not probable that his name was in any way responsible for the application of that title to Negro discriminatory laws introduced, first, in Tennessee in 1875. The title came, rather, from a popular song, copyrighted in 1828 by Thomas D. Rice, which became part of a skit, *The Rifle,* written by Solon Robinson. The song and its accompanying dance, it is said, were based on the chance observance of an old Negro in Louisville, Kentucky, who shuffled as he sang, "Weel about, turn about, do jist so." In the skit, produced in Washington in 1835 and taken to London in 1836, where it became equally popular, Rice, in black-face, sang, as he danced:

First on de heel tap, den on de toe,
Ebery time I wheel about I jump Jim Crow.
Wheel about and turn about and do jis so,
And ebery time I wheel about I jump Jim Crow.

fatten (or sweeten) the kitty

No, in modern usage at least, this "kitty" is not a member of the cat family. The expression is a gambling term, chiefly poker nowadays, and today means to increase the stakes, to add chips to an unopened jack pot. According to Hoyle, however, "kitty" is "the percentage taken out of the stakes in a game for expenses of any kind." In this connection it refers to the "take" of the house, whether the gambling be cards, pool, racing, or other sport. The source is by no means positive, but I suspect that someone with a fine sense of irony derived this "kitty" as the natural offspring of the "blind tiger" of faro fame. (See *A Hog on Ice*, page 82.)

to pull one's leg

To coax, wheedle, blarney; bamboozle, delude, pull the wool over one's eyes; befool, make fun of one. Our cousins over the seas, among whom the expression originated, use it in the latter senses; the first is an American addition, carrying the tomfoolery into downright cheating and chiseling. The Scots were apparently the first with the idea, using "draw" rather than "pull," as in the following quotation from a rhyme written in 1867:

He preached an' at last drew the auld body's leg,
Sae the kirk got the gatherins [the money] o' our Aunty Meg.

Just why one's leg was something to be either drawn or pulled for the success of a delusion is most uncertain. Perhaps it had something to do with tripping a person; i.e., to catch him in an error, or to bring him into a state of confusion.

to hide one's light under a bushel

To conceal one's talents or abilities; keep in the background; be unduly modest. This has reference to the fifth chapter of St. Matthew, in which, following the Beatitudes, Jesus called upon his disciples to be "the light of the world," adding, in the fourteenth and fifteenth verses, "A city that is set on a hill cannot be hid. Neither do men light a candle and put it under a bushel, but on a candlestick." ("Bushel," here, is the vessel used as a bushel measure.) But the preachers were already using this simile from earlier translations than the King James Version. It was used in 1557, and, not in the present sense of humility, in a sermon by Bishop Robert Sanderson in 1627, in which he said: "The light of God's word, hid from them under two bushels for sureness: under the bushel of a tyrannous clergy . . . and under the bushel of an unknown tongue."

to take a leaf out of one's book

If you do it figuratively, it's all right. The person whose leaf is thus taken is likely to feel flattered, if he learns of it, because the implied meaning is to imitate, to copy, to ape another person, as in deportment, manner, or method, etc. But if you do it literally and are caught at it, you run a good chance of running afoul of the law against plagarism. Nowadays you may not take another man's book, copy a leaf from it, or even a paragraph from that leaf, and publish it as your own. You may not even print it without due credit or his (or his publisher's) written permission. The penalty can be costly.

a nigger in the woodpile (or fence)

Some fact of considerable importance that is not disclosed; something suspicious or wrong; something rotten in Denmark. The sayings with "fence" and "woodpile" developed about the same time and about at the period, 1840–50, when the "Underground Railroad" was flourishing successfully. Evidence is slight, but because early uses of the expressions occurred in Northern states, it is presumable that they derived from actual instances of the surreptitious concealment of fugitive Negroes in their flight north through Ohio or Pennsylvania to Canada under piles of firewood or within hiding places in stone fences.

to toe the mark

To conform with the rules or to standards of discipline; to fulfil one's obligations; to come up to scratch. Literally, this used to be a term in footracing, now replaced by the command "Take your marks." An order, that is, to all entrants in a race to place the forward foot on the designated starting line. The expression does not appear to be more than about a hundred and fifty years old and could have been of American origin. At least the earliest use thus far found is in James K. Paulding's *The Diverting History of John Bull and Brother Jonathan* (New York, 1813).

cutting off one's nose to spite one's face

Injuring oneself in taking revenge upon another; damaging oneself through pique. Apperson has traced this back to a French saying that was current in the seventeenth century. Among the *Historiettes* of Gédéon Tallemant des Réaux, written about 1658,

 he finds: *"Henri iv conçut fort bien que détruire Paris, c'étoit, comme on dit, se couper le nez pour faire dépit à son visage"* (Henry IV well knew that to destroy Paris would be, as they say, to cut off his own nose in taking spite on his own face). Very likely there was some popular animal story similar to the account of *Reynard the Fox,* circulated by the troubadours of the Middle Ages, which told of a foolish creature that did, inadvertently, commit such an act, but the story has not come down to us, if it existed. But the French saying crossed the channel to England before the end of the eighteenth century and was recorded in Grose's *A Classical Dictionary of the Vulgar Tongue* (1796): "He cut off his nose to be revenged of his face. Said of one who, to be revenged on his neighbor, has materially injured himself."

to hit the nail on the head

To say or do the right thing; to express in words the exact idea; to speak to the point; to hit the bull's-eye. Our old Romans may have given us the grounds for this expression in the common saying, *acu rem tangere,* literally, "to touch a matter on the point," but which is ordinarily rendered, "to hit the nail on the head." For that matter, though the French say *mettre le doigt dessus,* "to hit on the finger," that too is ordinarily translated into our English saying. But our own expression goes back at least four and a half centuries. Apperson reports finding it in the *Vulgaria* (*c.* 1520) of John Stanbridge: "Thou hyttest the nayle on the head."

to stick one's neck out

To expose oneself to criticism; to take a chance, especially an extremely risky one; to monkey with the buzz saw. Although this American slang is of considerably later vintage, probably little more than thirty years old, it is my opinion that it arose also from the nineteenth-century slang, "to get it in the neck," or "to get it where the chicken got the ax." That is, as anyone who has beheaded chickens has learned, when the creature's head is placed upon the block the animal will usually stretch out its neck, thus making the butcher's aim more certain. Just some physiological reaction, I suppose. Of course, the expression could have originated from the victim of a lynching bee, but I do not think so.

to turn the tables

In my explanation of this expression in *A Hog on Ice* the assumption was made that it originated about three centuries ago from some unknown game of cards. The game from which the expression arose was backgammon, not cards. This is a game of considerable antiquity, thought to have been invented in the tenth century, but probably related to the game *Ludud duodecim scriptorum,* "twelve-line game," played in ancient Rome. In Chaucer's time and until the seventeenth century the game was invariably known as "tables" in England, and even in modern play the board is customarily divided into two (or four) "tables." The play is too involved to describe here, but there are often dramatic reversals of fortune due, not to reversing the position of the board, but to a rule which allows a player to double the stakes under certain circumstances—literally, to turn the tables. Sir St. Vincent Troubridge, to whom I am indebted for this correction, informs me that backgammon has again become popular in London social clubs and that stakes are sometimes very high.

snake in the grass

We owe this proverbial saying to the Roman poet Vergil (70–19 B.C.). In the third *Eclogue* is the line *Latet anguis in herba*, "A snake lurks in the grass." Apperson reports the appearance of this Latin proverb also in a political song in England round the year 1290: *Cum totum fecisse putas, latet anguis in herba*, "Though all appears clean, a snake lurks in the grass." The saying was used frequently thereafter. The earliest English translation was Edward Hall's *Chronicles* (1548): *The Union of the Two Noble and Illustre Famelies of Lancestre and Yorke*: "But the serpent lurked vnder the grasse, and vnder sugered speache was hide pestiferous poyson." The French put the snake under a rock, *quelque anguille sous roche*.

to bring (or put) under the hammer

It is the auctioneer's hammer that is meant, the small mallet used by him when tapping "once," to indicate that the item on sale is about to be "going" to the latest bidder; "twice," to give reluctant bidders another chance; "three times," as notice that the item has been "sold" or has "gone" to that latest bidder. The expression in present form goes back about a century and a half. For about an equal period before that the common expression was "to pass under, or sell at, the spear." This was translated from the Latin, *sub hasta vendere*, referring to the Roman custom of thrusting a spear into the ground at public auctions, the spear being a token of booty gained in battle and coming into the possession of the state.

to strain at a gnat and swallow a camel

To make a fuss over trifles but accept great faults without complaint. This, as are many others, is a Biblical expression. It is found in Matthew xxiii, 24–26: "Ye blind guides, which strain at a gnat and swallow a camel. Woe unto you, scribes and Pharisees, hypocrites! for ye make clean the outside of the cup and of the platter, but within they are full of extortion and excess. Thou blind Pharisee, cleanse first that which is within the cup and platter, that the outside of them may be clean also." But the translators of the King James

Bible of 1611 were already familiar with this figure of speech. It had appeared in *Lectures upon Jonas* by Bishop John King, first printed in 1594, reprinted in 1599, in which the bishop himself said, "They have verified the olde proverbe in strayning at gnats and swallowing downe camells."

to win one's spurs

To prove one's ability; to perform some deed by which one first gains honor among one's fellows. And there are a thousand ways by which it may be accomplished—a salesman by making his first sale, or his first important sale; a clergyman in delivering his first sermon; a doctor in attending his first patient; an author by the publication of his first story or book; an athlete by winning his first contest; or even, I suppose, by a yegg cracking his first safe. The allusion is to the young squire or princeling who, "when knighthood was in flower" in medieval days, had performed his first meritorious act or deed of valor by which he gained knighthood, by which his lord "dubbed" him a knight, tapping him with a sword lightly on the shoulder. After which accolade this lord or another presented the new member of the order with a pair of gilded spurs. Though early practices remain under discussion, this procedure, however, was apparently not adopted before the late fourteenth century. Thus we read in John Lydgate's *The Assembly of Gods* (c. 1425), "These xiiii knyghtes made Vyce that day; To wynne theyr spores they seyde they wold asay."

with tongue in cheek

This is something I'd like to see, or hear. Just how one can accomplish such a gymnastic lingual feat of lodging the tip or other portion of the tongue against the cheek and then uttering any distinguishable word is beyond my imagination. I can't do it. The English humorist, Richard Barham, seems to have dreamed up the feat. In *The Ingoldsby Legends* (1845), in the story of the "Black Mousquetaire," he has a Frenchman saying, " '*Superbe!—Magnifique!*' (With his tongue in his cheek.)" Perhaps that explains why I could never work up an interest in *The Ingoldsby Legends.* Other writers, however, have taken up the expression. Thus we have so eminent a writer as Matthew Arnold, in *Culture and Anarchy* (1869), saying, "He unquestionably knows that he is talking clap-trap, and, so to say, puts his tongue in his cheek." From this we infer that the one so performing engages in irony or insincerity.

to eat salt with (a person); **to eat** (a person's) **salt**

To be on terms of amity. From time immemorial the sharing of salt with another has been a sign of hospitality and, therefore, a token of friendship. Among the ancient Greeks, the oath taken "with salt and over the table" was held as an expression of sacred hospitality. The Arabs say, "there is salt between us." And, in the Revised Standard Version of the Bible, we read in Ezra, Chapter iv, how the enemies of the Hebrews went to the king and, in token of friendship, said to him, "Now because we eat the salt of the palace and it is not fitting for us to witness the king's dishonor . . . We make known to the king that, if this city [Jerusalem] is rebuilt and its walls finished, you will then have no possession in the province Beyond the River"—because it was certain that the Jews would rebel and pay no tribute.

keeping up with the Joneses

Though I have been regretfully obliged to abridge, I'll let Arthur R. ("Pop") Momand, the creator of this expression, now adopted into the American language, tell in his own words, from a personal letter to me, how it originated:

Here is how it happened: At the age of 23 I was making $125 a week (good money in those days, with no income tax). I married and moved to Cedarhurst, L.I., joined a country club, rode horseback daily, and bought a fifty-dollar bull-pup; also we kept a colored maid who, as I recall, had the glamorous name of Beatrice Montgomery. And we entertained in the grand manner, or as grand as we could on $125 a week. Well, it was not long until the butcher, the baker et al were knocking gently but firmly on the old front door. In the end we pulled up stakes, headed for New York and moved into a cheap apartment.

Our Cedarhurst experience was a rude awakening, but I saw the humorous side of it. We had been living far beyond our means in our endeavor to keep up with the well-to-do class which then lived in Cedarhurst. I also noted that most of our friends were doing the same; the $10,000-a-year chap was trying to keep up with the $20,000-a-year man.

I decided it would make good comic-strip material, so sat down and drew up six strips. At first I thought of calling it *Keeping up with the Smiths,* but finally decided on *Keeping up with the Joneses* as being more euphonious.

Taking the strips to The Associated Newspapers at 170 Broadway, I saw the manager, H. H. McClure. He appeared interested and asked me to give him a week to decide. In three days he phoned, saying they would sign a one-year contract for the strip. *Keeping up with the Joneses* was launched—and little did I realize it was to run for 28 years and take us across the Atlantic 42 times.

The feature was released in February of 1913 and appeared first in the New York *Globe,* Chicago *Daily News,* Boston *Globe,* Philadelphia *Bulletin* and ten minor papers. At that time I signed it POP, a nickname I had acquired at school. Later I signed the drawings POP MOMAND. In 1915 I had it copyrighted in my name. The strip gained in popularity each year; it appeared in 2-reel comedies, was put on as a musical comedy, and Cupples and Leon each year published a book of *Keeping up with the Joneses* cartoons. I have made the drawings in London, Paris, Berlin, Madrid, Vienna, Amsterdam, Los Angeles, and South America, mailing them to the Syndicate from wherever I chanced to be.

After 28 years on the old treadmill I tired of it. Today I paint portraits, landscapes, and marines—and, yes, I hate to admit it, we are still trying to keep up with the Joneses.

to cry wolf

There are, I suppose, as many versions of *Aesop's Fables* as there are publishers who have reprinted them with added tales from other sources. The version from which I took this story of "The Shepherd-boy and the Wolf" runs as follows:

A shepherd-boy who kept his flock a little way from a village for some time amused himself with this sport: he would call loudly on the villagers to come to his help, crying, "Wolf! wolf! the wolves are among my lambs!" Twice, three times the villagers were startled, and hurried out, and went back laughed at, when finally the wolves really did come. And as the wolves made way with the flock, and he ran crying for help, they supposed him only at his old joke, and paid no attention. And so he lost all his flock.

It only shows that people who tell lies get this for their pains, that nobody believes them when they speak the truth.

to shake a stick at

Although this does have a literal meaning, to threaten with a stick, we in the United States give it much more fanciful interpretations. If we say, "There are more filling stations in town than one can shake a stick at," we mean nothing more than that the town contains an abundance of places at which one may purchase gasoline for one's motorcar. That American usage dates from early in the nineteenth century. One may speculate that it arose from the play at warfare by small boys—George Washington Jones flourishing a triumphant wooden sword over the considerable number of British soldiers who surrendered at Yorktown, more, in fact, than he could wave his "stick" at. Then, too, we use the expression to indicate a comparative that may express derogation, and have done so for well over a hundred years. David Crockett, in his *Tour to the North and Down East* (1835), wrote of one place at which he stayed, "This was a temperance house, and there was nothing to treat a friend to that was worth shaking a stick at."

to sit above (or below) the salt

He who sits "above" is among the elect, honored, or socially acceptable; he who sits "below" is just an also-ran, an ordinary person, perhaps even inferior in social standing. The allusion is to the dining customs in the houses of the nobility and gentry in medieval days. The saltcellar (properly "saler")—a large container—was placed about the center of the table and all guests of distinction were ranged in order of merit at the upper or master's end of the table "above" the salt, or saltcellar. The dependents, tenants, or persons of low degree sat "below" the salt, or at the lower end of the table. The prolific writer, Bishop Joseph Hall, in Book II of his *Satires* (1597), tells us:

> A gentle Squire would gladly entertaine
> Into his House some trencher-chapelaine,
> Some willing man that might instruct his Sons,
> And that could stand to good Conditions:
> First that He lie vpon the Truckle-bed,

Whiles his yong maister lieth ore his hed;
Second that he do, on no default,
Euer presume to sit aboue the salt. . . .

like a bear with a sore head

Very disgruntled; peevish; ill-tempered; soreheaded. Professor
Hans Sperber of Ohio State University, in his studies of words and
phrases in American politics, argues that the American term "sorehead," meaning a disgruntled person, is derived from the metaphor,

 "like a bear with a sore head" (*American
Speech,* Vol. XXVII). To add point to
the argument he cites some uses of a century and more ago: Cincinnati *Gazette,*
October 26, 1824, "The engineer, Daw-
son, a pussy fatwitted Irishman, was rav-
ing round the forecastle like a bear with
a sore head, ever and anon vociferating
corruption," and W. G. Simms, *The Parti-
san* (1835), "Art thou, now, not a sorry
bear with a sore head, that kindness cannot coax, and crossing only
can keep civil!" Then he goes on through the years with other
quotations which lend support to his contention that the "bear with
a sore head" became the source of the political term, "sorehead,"
used first in the campaign of 1848, "when the opponents of the
newly founded Free Soil party characterized it as a motley crowd
recruited from the refuse of other parties," demonstrated by a quotation from the Albany *Weekly Argus,* August 12th of that year:
"As no other selection could be supposed so well to represent such
a conventicel [sic] of 'sore heads,' it is perhaps quite as well it
sho'd take direction as any other."

Although Professor Sperber modestly admits that he has indulged
in a certain amount of guesswork in his etymology, his circumstan-
tial evidence is nevertheless convincing. Regrettably, the origins of
slang and colloquial expressions are rarely recorded at birth; consequently, later researchers are often obliged to resort to conjecture.

But Professor Sperber assumes in his discussion that the expression, "a bear with a sore head," grew out of the experience of hunt-

ers who learned that shooting a bear in the head was likely to lead to nothing more than to make the animal truculent, highly irascible and fighting mad. I doubt that explanation, though it stands to reason that any animal, bear or other, so injured by a non-fatal shot would not be exactly jovial. I suggest, therefore, though I have no record to prove it, that the metaphor arose belatedly either from bear-baiting, in which dogs were set upon a bear chained to a stake, or from the ancient tales of *Reynard the Fox.* You will recall that one of these tales relates how Reynard greatly discomfited Bruin by leading him to a succulent repast of honey, which, however, was stored in a cleft of a tree. When Bruin inserted his head to gorge upon the honey, the fox slyly removed the wedge left by the woodsman, and then led the farmer to the scene. Bruin made his escape only at the expense of losing most of the skin from his head, and was indeed "a bear with a sore head" when he returned to court.

hair and hide (horns and tallow)

The whole works; every part; the entirety. The first part, hair and hide, has long been used in the same sense. In fact, five hundred years ago, in the metrical *Life of St. Cuthbert,* we find: "Þai were destroyed, bath hare and hyde." The second part, horns and tallow, is, I suspect, a fairly recent American additive probably of the wild-woolly-West school of literature to impress youthful readers. When the earlier part is reversed and used negatively, as in "I have seen neither hide nor hair of the cat since yesterday," the sense is that the speaker hasn't seen any part of the animal, and this usage dates back apparently little more than a century.

hold your horses

Don't be in too great a hurry; take it easy; watch your step; keep your shirt on; be patient; control your temper. This homely admonition traces back to the American county fair of old, to the races which, among the menfolk especially, were the main features of the day. The harness races were especially difficult to get started, for the horses, sensing the tautness of inexperienced eager drivers, were constantly breaking from the line and had to be called back. Figurative transfer to human restiveness and its restraint was but a step.

As early as 1844 we find in the old *New Orleans Picayune*, "Oh, hold your hosses, Squire. There's no use gettin' riled, no how."

itching palm

A wistful desire for money; a hankering for gain; avariciousness; readiness to receive a bribe. Other bodily parts were metaphorically said to itch, even before Shakespeare's time—such as an "itching tongue," a craving to repeat gossip; an "itching ear," a craving to hear something new; an "itching foot," a craving for travel. But Shakespeare gave us the "itching palm." It is to be found in *Julius Caesar* (1601), Act IV, scene 3. Cassius has come to the tent of Brutus to voice certain complaints, especially to criticize Brutus for condemning a friend of Cassius for taking bribes. In reply Brutus says: "Let me tell you, Cassius, you your selfe Are much condemn'd to haue an itching Palme."

to stick (or put) in one's oar (in another's boat)

To enter without invitation into the affairs of another; to interfere or meddle; to butt into a conversation or the like; to add one's two-cents' worth. There's no telling where this originated. Its first appearance in English is in the *Apophthegmes, That is to Saie, Prompte Saiynges* (1542), translated by Nicolas Udall from the collection, in Latin, of adages garnered by Erasmus, published in 1500. In Udall's translation it is thus given:

> Whatsoeuer came in his foolyshe brain,
> Out it should, wer it neuer so vain.
> In eche mans bote would he haue an ore,
> But no woorde, to good purpose, lesse or more.

Along in the eighteenth century the "boat" phrase was occasionally dropped, and we in America now use "stick" more frequently than either "put" or "have."

to get it in the neck

To get it where the chicken got the ax; to be defeated or punished; to be on the carpet; also, to be deceived. The first definition, in its literal sense, adequately explains the origin of this American slang, and the first definition used figuratively is fully synonymous with each of the other meanings. The expression is at least seventy years old, first reported in the Louisville (Kentucky) *Courier,* issue of January 20, 1887. The report dealt with the play, *The James Boys,* at the New Buckingham Theatre the previous Saturday evening. The galleries were filled with bootblacks, newsboys, and small boys generally. As half a dozen dark-visaged and heavily armed rogues crept on the darkened stage and gathered around a barrel marked in large white letters "Powder," one small urchin in a most excited stage whisper said, according to the reporter, "Dem dubs is goin' to get it in de neck in a minit."

casting pearls before swine

"Give not that which is holy unto the dogs, neither cast ye your pearls before swine, lest they trample them under their feet, and turn again and rend you." That is the sixth verse of the seventh chapter of Matthew. Of the passage John Wyclif wrote in 1380: "Þus [Thus] comaundeth crist þat men schullen not yeve [give] holy þingis to hondis [hounds] & putten precious perles to hoggis." That is, grandmother, don't bequeath the most revered among your treasured antiques to a daughter or daughter-in-law who cares only for modernistic décor, and, granddad, no matter how generous your instincts, you are merely casting pearls before swine in giving your six-year-old grandson a set of ivory chessmen at Christmas, rather than lead Indians.

to keep the pot boiling

To provide for one's living; to keep at gainful employment that will produce income; also, to keep interest from flagging; to keep the ball rolling. In former times when gentlemen and ladies were not supposed to work, to sell their time and effort for wages, some still found it necessary to produce some sort of salable commodity in order to continue to eat. It was genteel, not vulgar labor, to write or to paint, and many a man in the early nineteenth century especially (and from then to the present time) kept food in his domestic pot and a fire under it, through the judicious exercise of these talents and the generosity of a benefactor. Thus we find

William Combe, himself a "potboiler" through long practice, in *The Tour of Doctor Syntax in Search of the Picturesque* (1812), saying in his customary doggerel: "No fav'ring patrons have I got, But just enough to boil the pot."

something rotten in Denmark

Something of a highly suspicious nature; a nigger in the woodpile; something likely to be corrupt. We have it from Shakespeare's *Hamlet,* Act I, scene 4. Hamlet has been summoned by the ghost of his father, the murdered king of Denmark, into a conversation apart from his friends Horatio and Marcellus. His friends urge him not to go alone, for fear of injury, but Hamlet insists and will not be denied, saying, "Unhand me, gentlemen, By heaven, I'll make a ghost of him that lets me," and departs with the ghost. Marcellus then says, "Let's follow; 'tis not fit thus to obey him." Horatio replies, "Have after. To what issue will this come?" To which Marcellus responds, "Something is rotten in the state of Denmark."

to crash the gate

If Willy Smith, in fitting attire, enters the portals of Madame Astorbilt's house or grounds, to which he has not been invited, in order to mingle with her party guests, he has "crashed the gate" to do so. Or if little red-haired Sammy Jones finds a way to sneak past a ticket-taker at the Polo Grounds or Madison Square Garden, he too "crashes the gate." Neither one has literally crashed anything— other than social or legal convention—but such an entrance, uninvited or non-paid, has been popular American designation since, approximately, the end of World War I. No one knows and there is no clue to the person who became the first *gate-crasher.*

to get in one's hair

To have someone or something persistently annoy one; to become greatly irked. I doubt that this American expression was of Western origin, though its first reported appearance was in the *Oregon Statesman* in 1851: "I shall depend on your honor . . . that you won't tell on me, cause if you did, I should have Hetty Gawkins in my hair in no time." But there had been towns and villages in that territory for almost forty years by that time, so it is of course possible that the expression signified some annoying Oregonian factor that actually did get in one's hair. What that annoyance may have been, we are not told. Nevertheless since body lice were then regarded as a more or less necessary evil, it is certainly within the realms of probability that these were the pests of the early reference, literally irritating the scalp.

to cry for the moon

"Breathes there a man with soul so dead" that he has never done this! Any such would be utterly lacking in either desire or ambition, one who goes through life just a-settin' like a Stoughton bottle. That is, we all, at some time, strive for the impossible or the unattainable—and, perhaps, the disappointment over our inability to answer the siren's call or to catch up with the will-o'-the-wisp inclines us to follow the lover in Lord Tennyson's *The Princess* (1847): "I babbled for you, as babies for the moon." It was Charles Dickens, however, who, in *Bleak House* (1852), was the first to put on record the present saying, even though, undoubtedly, the babies of Adam and Eve and all babies since must have reached out their plump little hands and demanded, in no uncertain tones, that the pretty yellow ball in the sky be placed therein. Dickens, describing in Chapter VI the actions of Mr. Skimpole, had him say of himself, "Give him the papers, conversation, music, mutton, coffee, landscape, fruit in the season, a few sheets of Bristol-board, and a little claret, and he asked no more. He was a mere child in the world, but he didn't cry for the moon."

to skate over (or on) thin ice

To approach or treat a delicate subject without causing offense; to risk imprudence or indelicacy in language. The author, in fact, has skated over thin ice several times in this book in his attempt to explain one or another irreligious or indecent expression tactfully, without giving occasion to any reader to drop the book in the fire. The allusion is to the sport indulged in by daredevil boys and venturesome young men, in winter, in skating rapidly over newly formed ice on lakes or streams, ice so thin that it would not bear his weight if the skater stopped or slowed down; hence, the risk of being plunged into icy water. In my own youth, as in that of my sons in New England, the sport was called "tickledy-bendo," partly from the bending ice as the skater skimmed its surface. The expression also is used to mean to undertake a venturesome enterprise, especially one relying upon consummate skill or great luck.

to ride the goat

To be initiated or inducted into an organization, especially into a secret society. In all probability, although no facts are ever likely to be disclosed, this expression actually did arise from the practice in some college Greek-letter fraternity of introducing a goat into the hazing of prospective candidates for membership. But the earliest record of the phrase occurs in *Peck's Bad Boy and His Pa* (1883), by George Wilbur Peck. In Chapter XIX, "His Pa Is 'Nishiated," the bad boy and his chum train a goat to butt a bockbeer sign, borrowed from a neighboring saloon, and ask "Pa" if he would like to be " 'nishiated" into their lodge and take "the bumper degree." When "Pa" agrees, he is told to "come up pretty soon and give three distinct raps, and when we asked him who come there must say 'A pilgrim who wants to join your ancient order and ride the goat.' " The goat, as the bad boy says, is "loaded for bear," and when "Pa" repeats the order, "Bring forth the Royal Bumper and let him Bump," the goat, seeing the bock-beer sign pinned to "Pa's" back side, lets him have it with the best "bump" of which he is capable.

to lead one up (or down) the garden (or garden path)

This expression, in frequent use by English writers, has not yet gained much currency in the United States. It is relatively new, dating probably no further back than around the end of World War I. When I wrote to Sir St. Vincent Troubridge, whom I have quoted variously elsewhere, to inquire whether he could suggest a possible origin, I advanced the theory that seduction might have been the aim in the "leading." He did not agree with that view, though he was not able to offer anything more plausible. Nevertheless, to quote the *Supplement* (1933) to *The Oxford English Dic-*

tionary, the saying means "to lead on, entice, mislead," and the earliest printed quotation that is cited is from Ethel Mannin's *Sounding Brass* (1926): "They're cheats, that's wot women are! Lead you up the garden and then go snivellin' around 'cos wot's natcheral 'as 'appened to 'em." If that doesn't imply seduction, then what does it imply? Be that as it may, current usage rarely, if ever, carries other meaning than to bamboozle, to hoax, to blarney, to pull one's leg, to deceive.

other fish to fry

The French idea is *il a bien d'autres chiens à fouetter,* literally, "he has many other dogs to whip." The Germans, with no frills, give the actual meaning—*andere Dinge zu tun haben,* "to have other things to do," as do the Italians with *altro pel capo.* The Spaniards are equally direct though your translated version of *Don Quixote* may give you a different idea. Thus, in the Motteux translation (1712), part II, chapter XXXV, Merlin tells the noble Don that the only way by which "the peerless Dulcinea del Toboso" may be disenchanted is that Sancho—

> ". . . thy good Squire,
> On his bare brawny buttocks should bestow
> Three thousand Lashes, and eke three hundred more,
> Each to afflict, and sting, and gall him sore."

But Sancho, quite naturally, objects to being the recipient of such indignity; the disenchantment of the fair Duchess is of no immediate concern to him; hence, " 'I say, as I have said before,' quoth Sancho; 'as for the flogging, I pronounce it flat and plain.' 'Renounce, you mean,' said the Duke. 'Good your Lordship,' quoth Sancho, 'this is no Time for me to mind Niceties, and spelling of Letters: I have other Fish to fry. . . .' "

Cervantes actually wrote, *otras cosas en que pensar,* "other things on which to think," but Motteux, anxious to show off his acquaintance with English idiom, adopted the phrase already well known. Just how old the "fish" version may be is not known. The first appearance in print that has yet been found is in the *Memoirs* (1660) of the prolific writer John Evelyn. Undoubtedly, however, it had long been familiar to his readers.

unable to see the wood for the trees

Too beset by petty things to appreciate greatness or grandeur; too wrapped up in details to gain a view of the whole. In America we are likely to use the plural, "woods," or possibly to substitute "forest," but "wood" is the old form and is preferable. Yes, the saying is at least five hundred years old, and probably a century or two could be added to that, for it must have long been in use to have been recorded in 1546 in John Heywood's *A Dialogue Conteynyng the Number in Effect of all the Prouerbes in the Englishe Tongue.* He wrote: "Plentie is no deinte, ye see not your owne ease. I see, ye can not see the wood for trees." And a few years later, in 1583, Brian Melbancke, in *Philotimus: the Warre Betwixt Nature and Fortune,* wrote: "Thou canst not or wilt not see wood for trees." The saying has cropped up repeatedly from then to the present, becoming, in fact, more frequent with the passing years.

son of a gun

Nowadays this is likely to be a respectable or nice-Nelly substitute for an epithet of the when-you-call-me-that-Smile variety, a male offspring of the female of the canine family. But it is also used as a term of affectionate regard, as between pals. In general, however, it is the opposite extreme, accompanied usually by a derogatory adjective and used as a term of contempt. It has been in the language for at least two and a half centuries, and if one is willing to accept the story of its origin given by Admiral William Henry Smyth of the British navy in *The Sailor's Word-Book,* written about 1865, here it is: "An epithet conveying contempt in a slight degree, and originally applied to boys born afloat, when women were permitted to accompany their husbands to sea; one admiral declared he literally was thus cradled, under the breast of a gun-carriage."

hot dog

It would have been my guess that this term for the popular American comestible came into circulation, along with the item itself, during the great Columbian Exposition in Chicago in 1893. But the New York *Herald Tribune,* in an editorial, "The Hot-Dog

Mystery," June 2, 1931, was not able to carry the date earlier than 1900. It hardly seems necessary to explain that the name itself is applied to a frankfurter, a highly seasoned sausage of mixed meats, usually grilled and placed in a split roll, the name being suggested by the one-time notion that the sausage was made of dog meat. The *Herald Tribune* credited the invention of the concoction to one, Harry M. Stevens, caterer at the New York Polo Grounds, who at that time heated not only the frankfurter but also the roll. However, Stevens, as reported by the *Herald Tribune* in his obituary, May 4, 1934, credited the name to the late T. A. Dorgan (known as "Tad," from his initials), a sports cartoonist, though unable to recall the date. In more recent days "hot dog" has become an ejaculation expressive of surprise or approval.

to give one the gate

This might appear to be a descendant of a saying of the fifteenth century, "to grant one the gate," as in *The Knightly Tale of Golagros and Gawane*: "The king grantit the gait to schir Gawane, And prayt to the grete Dod to grant him his grace." That is to say, the king granted Sir Gawane permission to leave, to pass through the gate and to take to the road. But that expression died many years ago. Ours is of twentieth-century birth and is reasonably literal in that it means to show one the door; hence, to give one his walking papers, or, that is, to dismiss a person, give him a walkout powder, give him the air, or, in baseball terminology, to send a player to the showers, retire him from the game.

by hook or by crook

By fair means or foul; in one way or another. As stated in *A Hog on Ice,* this expression is so old, dating back at least to the four-teenth century, that, though many derivations have been advanced, no certainty of origin has been obtained. This statement brought a letter from Admiral Gerald J. FitzGerald of Chicago, which I am privileged to quote, and to which was attached a clipping: "Admiral Gerald J. FitzGerald—of the Knight of Glin branch, of the Lord (Earl) of Desmond branch, of the House of Geraldine—can trace his pedigree back to Adam and Eve."

In regard to "by hook or by crook," Admiral FitzGerald wrote: "The origin has an affinity with my family . . . When my ancestors, the FitzGerald barons, were invading Ireland around A.D. 1169–1170, it was decided to establish a beachhead at Waterford because of its excellent harbor. As the invading squadrons were cruising across the broad expanse of water, they saw on the Emerald Isle's left shore a lofty tower, and on the right a magnificent church. A spy was asked what these places were and he responded, 'On the left, the Tower of Hook, and on the right, the Church of Crook.' 'Then,' said the head lord and marshal, 'we'll invade and take this great Kingdom of Ireland by Hook or Crook.' "

This account has at least the novelty of differing from all the others that I have seen, and history does record the fact that Gerald, ancestor of the FitzGerald family, was among the Anglo-Norman leaders authorized by Henry II of England to invade Ireland.

a leap in the dark

Any undertaking the outcome of which cannot be foreseen; a venture of uncertain consequence. At least, such are the modern interpretations, and we apply the metaphor to just about anything we have under contemplation of which the consequences cannot be determined. But the earliest usage of which we have record gives the phrase a more sinister interpretation. That is, in Sir John Vanbrugh's *The Provok'd Wife* (1697), we find (Act V, scene 6), the words of one dying, "So, now, I am in for Hobbes voyage, a great leap in the dark." The allusion being that the English philosopher, Thomas Hobbes, 1588–1679, on his deathbed was alleged to have said, "Now I am about to take my last voyage, a great leap in the dark."

paying (or working) for a dead horse

Performing work for which payment has already been made; ergo, doing something which is no longer profitable. I have no doubt that the Greeks had a phrase for this, and the Egyptians before them, and so on back to the first time that man worked for hire— or at least to the first one who got paid in advance. Nothing is quite so irksome. The allusion, of course, is to that unfortunate man who at some remote period bought a horse to work his field only to have the animal die before the field was sown—and the animal still to be paid for. A modern parallel is to buy a car on time, only to wreck it before the second payment has been made. Literary record of the English phrase has been traced back to the seventeenth century.

to do (put on, pull, or play) the baby act

To act in a manner typical of a baby; that is, to whine, coax, wheedle, shed tears, yell, howl, scream, kick, or otherwise adopt a babylike action in order to evoke sympathy, gain attention, or get one's way; as, "He weakened when she pulled the baby act, for he couldn't stand tears." The expression in  any of its forms is modern, but the act itself undoubtedly traces back to Eve, who was the first female determined to have her own way. But the small boy also puts on the baby act when he thinks he may gain something thereby, and perhaps occasionally his older brother, for the act is not altogether confined to the female of the species.

This expression should not be confused with the phrase, "to plead the baby act." Here the defense may be (a) that a contract is legally void because it was entered into by one still a minor, or (b) that the person committing a stupid act was so ignorant or inexperienced as to warrant excuse. Thus, for example, a person who entered a Communist cell while in college may later "plead the baby act" on the grounds that, because of the inexperience of youth, he was not then legally responsible.

to flog a dead horse

To try to revive a feeling of interest that has died; to engage in a fruitless undertaking. The French express it more literally—*chercher à ressusciter un mort*, to seek to resuscitate a corpse. But whatever the language, the sense is clear: it is as useless to try to stir up interest in an issue that is dead as it would be to try to get a dead horse to pull a load by flogging it.

to wait for dead men's shoes

Though "deadman" may have a variety of meanings—a corpse; a log, concrete block, or other heavy mass buried in the ground to serve as an anchor; an empty liquor bottle, "dead soldier"; a timber, in logging, to which the hawser of a boom is attached—we are concerned with something more literal here. These shoes belong to a man still living which the one who is waiting is anxious to try on for size if only the "old geezer" would pass along to his final reward. Sometimes the "shoes" mean the job to which one hopes to succeed, or they may mean the possessions or title that will descend to one. The saying is old. It was recorded in John Heywood's *A Dialogue Conteynyng the Nomber in Effect of All the Prouerbes in the Englishe Tongue* (1546)—"Who waiteth for dead men shoen, shall go long barefoote"—and, therefore, is undoubtedly much older.

the daughter of the horseleech

"The horseleech hath two daughters, crying, Give, give." You will find that in Proverbs, xxx, 15. Of course, the horseleech is an aquatic sucking worm, of large size and great sucking facilities which veterinary surgeons of old employed to remedy common diseases of the horse; hence, the name. But the name, as far back as the sixteenth century, was therefore also applied to any veterinary surgeon and, because of the natural propensities of the worm itself, to any rapacious insatiable person, to any bloodsucker, clinging to another and robbing him of money, ideas, or other resources. His daughters, presumably, are even more grasping; hence, any "daughter of a horseleech" is anyone, especially any female, who is constantly crying, "Give, give."

to ride for a fall

To lose intentionally; also, to fail in an enterprise. Obviously the saying stems from horse racing, especially in a steeplechase, in which a rider, though on a favorite mount, deliberately rides in such manner as to disqualify himself by, apparently, being thrown from his horse. The expression—recent American—has been transferred to other contests and games in which one of the contestants or contesting sides deliberately, but very slyly, loses the contest. However, the expression has also been employed in a sense not at all sinister. Any person who embarks upon an undertaking—commercial, amorous, or whatever—that seems doomed to fail, is also said to be riding for a fall.

to throw the book at one

Many a man who has had "the book" thrown at him would infinitely prefer that it had been a literal book, no matter how large or hefty. But no, it is a figurative book, or, rather, the contents of a literal book. Originally, and usually, "the book" is the maximum sentence that a judge can legally impose upon one convicted of a crime, and is often interpreted to mean life imprisonment. However, the metaphor has now been taken into non-criminal slang and is variously interpreted. In military circles, for instance, it usually implies a severe sentence resulting from a court martial, but it also may mean nothing more serious than a stiff reprimand from a superior officer. In family circles, father may "throw the book at" an erring son or daughter by depriving him or her of certain privileges. The expression appears to be of American origin, but, as with most criminal argot, its history is dubious.

fly-by-night

Quite properly, anyone who is a "fly-by-night" is one who decamps secretly or who departs hurriedly or clandestinely, usually at night, from a scene of recent activity, as from solicitous creditors or from anxious purchasers of worthless mining stocks or the like. In any case, he is a four-flusher, a swindler, and his activities are fraudulent. But the term originally had a literal meaning, or at least a meaning that its users thought to be literal. Even so recently as a century and a half ago it meant a witch, one who, as popularly supposed, actually mounted her broom or besom at midnight and went off on her round of appointments, whatever they may have been, or to meet secretly the Old Boy himself.

to put the finger on someone

This American slang has a far different connotation than the older "to put (or lay) one's finger upon something." The latter, though in general use the past hundred years, has the specific meaning, to point out, to indicate precisely; especially to show meaning or cause. But the newer expression is gutter slang for "to mark a person for murder," or "to accuse one of being a stool-pigeon," or, somewhat with the older meaning, "to inform on a person."

Davy Jones's locker

Maybe there was once an Englishman whose name was really Davy Jones. Perhaps he was the barman of the sixteenth-century ballad, "Jones Ale Is Newe," and the locker, dreaded by seamen, may have been where he stored his ale. That is speculation, how-ever. Actually the source of the name and the reason for bestowing it upon the bottom of the sea, especially as the grave of those who have perished in the sea—"gone to Davy Jones's locker"—cannot be fathomed. The first mention of Davy Jones—his locker came later—is to be found in *The Adventures of Peregrine Pickle,* writ-ten by Tobias Smollett in 1751. It occurs in the episode (Chapter XIII) describing the attempt by Peregrine and his two associates to frighten Commodore Trunnion by a dread apparition they have prepared, succeeding so well that the commodore exclaims:

"By the Lord! Jack, you may say what you wool; but I'll be damned if it was not Davy Jones himself. I know him by his saucer eyes, his three rows of teeth, and tail, and the blue smoke that came out of his nostrils. What does the black-guard hell's baby want with me? . . ."

This same Davy Jones [Smollet adds], according to the mythology of sailors, is the fiend that presides over all the evil spirits of the deep, and is often seen in various shapes, perching among the rigging on the eve of hurricanes, ship-wrecks, and other disasters to which sea-faring life is exposed, warning the devoted wretch of death and woe.

to get one's dander up

To get angry; to become riled or ruffled. Dad gets his dander up when neighbor Simpson implies that his new Chevvy runs better than dad's new Ford, but he also gets his dander up, good and plenty, when son Pete smashes a fender of that same Ford backing into a tree. *Dander* still means "anger" in the dialectal speech of several English counties, but the full phrase appears to be entirely

American. In the dialectal use we find it in Seba Smith's *The Life and Writings of Major Jack Downing, of Downingville* (1830–33), a book dedicated to General Andrew Jackson. In "Letter LXV," dated July 20, 1833, the Major tells about a quarrel between him and Mr. Van Buren at Concord, in which Van Buren belittles the major's qualifications for the presidency. "At this," says the Major, "my dander began to rise . . ."

Through the popularity of these humorous yarns and letters, Smith began to have several imitators. The most pretentious was Charles A. Davis, who, in 1834, brought out *Letters of J. Downing, Major, Downingville Militia, Second Brigade*. In the third "letter," after describing a dance, in which "Gineral" Jackson participated, the fictitious Downing goes on to say that several of the men, including Van Buren, then tried on Jackson's coat, after he had retired: "Then cum my turn; but I see how the cat jump'd, 'so,' says I, 'I'll jest step out and rig in another room:' and I went strait to the Gineral, and woke him up, and tell'd him all about it—he was wrathy as thunder—and when he gets his dander up, it's no joke, I tell you."

Hence, to Davis, rather than to Smith, goes the credit, for what it may amount to, for being the first to record this expression. Probably, however, it was a popular phrase of the period, as shortly thereafter it appeared in the works of other writers, among them, Colonel David Crockett in his *Life* (1835) and upon the lips of "Sam Slick" in Thomas Haliburton's *The Clockmaker* (1837–40).

weasel words

Slaps on the wrist; words that weaken or detract from the effectiveness or force of another word or expression. The expression is often erroneously accredited to Theodore Roosevelt. He did use it and define it, however, in a speech at St. Louis, May 31, 1916. Roosevelt, along with many others, thought that action, rather than chidings, should be taken by the Wilson administration for the depredations by the German navy on American shipping. He said the notes from the Department of State were filled with "weasel words," adding, "When a weasel sucks eggs the meat is sucked out of the egg. If you use a 'weasel word' after another there is nothing left of the other." But the expression first appeared in an article, "The Stained-Glass Political Platform," by Stewart Chaplin, in the June, 1900, issue of *Century Magazine*. In the course of the dialogue in which the article is written, one St. John, reading the "platform" aloud, quoted, " 'the public should be protected—' 'Duly protected' said Gamage. 'That's always a good weasel word.' "

to burn one's boats (or bridges)

To make retreat impossible; hence, figuratively, to make a categorical statement or to take a positive stand from which none but an ignominious withdrawal is possible. I have read that this expression with the "boat" terminus was an ancient Greek idiom, but if that is true I have not been able to find it. However, the literal burning of his boats after crossing rivers or seas with his armies into alien lands was a practice of Caesar's to make his leaders and men realize most definitely that a victorious campaign would offer the only chance of a safe return to Rome. In much later periods the generals of invading armies had bridges burned behind them with the same object, as well as to add difficulties to pursuers.

willing to give one's ears

Willing to make a marked sacrifice. The allusion is to a punishment for certain crimes in the England of the twelfth century and later—and in America, too—by which one or both ears of him or her adjudged to be guilty were cut off. But though the punishable crimes run on back through the centuries, our present expression itself is not much more than a hundred years old. Hence, it must be left to the imagination which of those various crimes—forgery, quackery, treason, adultery, and others—could have been so desirable as to make one willing to suffer such an undesirable penalty.

to throw (or cast) dust in one's eyes

The ancient Romans expressed this same thought by saying, "*verba dare alicui*," which, translated, is "to give empty words," and that is what we do when we throw dust in anyone's eyes. We say a lot of empty words or perform some action which will confuse or mislead that person, blinding him, as it were, to actual facts.

Probably the generals of ancient armies took advantage of nature's own dust storms, whenever possible, to conceal the movements of their forces. But the earliest instance of an English phrase similar to present-day usage is to be found in the translation by George Pettie (1581) of Guazzo's *Ciuilie Conuersation* (*Civil Conversation*): "They doe nothing else but raise a dust to doe out their owne eies." However, one form of the modern phrase appears in Thomas Birch's *The Court and Times of James the First,* published before 1766: "He [Salisbury, lord treasurer] found so little good at the Bath, that he made all the haste that he could out of that suffocating, sulphurous air, as he called it, though others think he hastened the faster homeward to countermine his underminers, and, as he termed it, to cast dust in their eyes."

hitting below the belt

Using unfair methods or actions. As anyone knows who has attended a prize fight or watched one on television, or who has witnessed any other pugilistic engagement, to strike one's opponent below the line of his belt is a foul blow and, if done deliberately or repeatedly, may cause the decision to be rendered against the offender. Both literal and figurative uses of the expression arose from the adoption in 1867 of the Marquis of Queensberry rules covering prize fighting.

tarred and feathered

Subjected to indignity and infamy. Not so long ago, and perhaps in some localities even yet, this was literal, a punishment or condemnation meted out upon someone adjudged to have merited such treatment. In its severest form the victim was stripped, sometimes shaved, and melted or even hot tar was poured or smeared over his head and body and he was then rolled in chicken feathers. The victim might then be ridden out of town on a rail or driven out by dogs. The punishment was first inflicted in England in 1189 by Richard I for one guilty of theft in the navy, but had been practiced in Europe in earlier years. In America a royal officer of the customs was tarred and feathered in Boston in 1774, and other Royalists, according to report, received similar treatment by hot-headed rebellious mobs in that period. The Ku Klux Klan and various American mobs repeatedly resorted to such measures in more recent years in attempts to rid a community of persons deemed by them to be undesirable.

to save (or lose) face

To maintain (or lose) one's dignity, prestige, or at least a semblance of such dignity or prestige or esteem before others; to avoid humiliation or disgrace. The Chinese use only *tiu lien,* which means "to lose face," though they have another expression, "for the sake of his face." It was the English residing in China who coined "to save face," and it is that expression, along with "to save one's face," that is in more common use among Occidentals than the translation of the phrase used by the Chinese themselves.

to draw (or pull) chestnuts from the fire

To be made a cat's-paw, to be used for the advantage of another. The story dates back at least to Pope Julius II (1503–1513) who, some say, owned the monkey of the tale. As related by Drexelius (in Latin, translated for me by Miss Phyllis L. Bolton), it reads:

I am told by an excellent and reliable man that there once was a monkey who, because he was a favored pet, ran free about his master's house. One day a soldier stood outside hungrily gazing into the kitchen. The cook pretended not to see him and failed to make the customary offering. Seeing his hopes frustrated, the soldier slipped into the kitchen and, the moment the cook disappeared, stepped to the hearth. As it happened, there were chestnuts roasting on the hearth and their fragrance, which had attracted the hungry watcher, was equally alluring to the monkey. He, too, was drawn to the fireplace where he beheld the cause of the enticing aroma and endeavored to pull them out of the coals. Failing sadly, unable to stand the heat, the monkey snatched back his singed fingers. At a loss what to do then, he sat scratching his head. Suddenly his eye fell upon the cat lying in wait for mice. In an instant he pounced upon her and forced her, struggling and spitting, to serve as his deputy. Seizing the cat's paw in his, he used it to draw one chestnut after another from the fire. The cat did not, naturally, take such servitude kindly, and back arched, fur on end, she howled piteously until her wails brought the cook to the rescue.

to get (or be given) the bounce

To be summarily ejected, as Polly Prim might say; to be ejected forcibly, as by a "bouncer," one employed to get troublesome characters—drunks, noisy persons, or the like—out of a saloon, bar, hotel, etc.; also, to be dismissed from employment, to be expelled  from membership in an organization or from attendance in some institution, or to be rejected as a suitor, etc.; in short, to be shown that one is not wanted. Apparently we Americans borrowed the expression, in translation, from the Dutch in some manner. At least, the Dutch have the phrase, *de bons geven,* "to give the bounce," which is employed to mean to jilt, dismiss, give the sack. We've had "bouncers" who performed the above-mentioned duties, since the days of the Civil War, but "bounce"—usually exaggerated to "grand bounce"—is recent American slang. Perhaps orally the expression itself, in one form or other, dates back to that period also, but literary usage carries it back only to O. Henry's story, "The Friendly Call," first published in *Monthly Magazine Section*, July, 1910. The story is about two friends who are always on tap to rescue one another from predicaments: Bell, who tells the story, went to the rescue of George from the attentions of a widow, asking Bell "to get her off his tail." Bell asks, "Had you ever thought of repressing your fatal fascinations in her presence; of squeezing a hard note in the melody of your siren voice, of veiling your beauty—in other words, of giving her the bounce yourself?"

to get one's Dutch up

To get one's dander up; to arouse one's temper. The reference is, of course, to the Pennsylvania Dutch, to the people of Germanic origin who, in the early seventeenth century, fled from continued religious persecutions in the Palatinate, chiefly, and brought their brands of Protestant faith into the sanctuary provided by William Penn in eastern Pennsylvania. They were a peaceful people, these paternal ancestors of mine. And they practiced their religion. Accordingly, they were slow to anger, keeping their tempers under subjugation. Nevertheless, so the historian Bancroft tells us, although representing only one-twelfth of the population at the time, the Pennsylvania Dutch composed one-eighth of the army in the Revolutionary War. And, from personal experience, I can vouch for the fact that some of their descendants, at least, had flaring tempers—although they might not let "the sun descend upon their wrath."

to go in at (or off) the deep end

This is variously interpreted. In England, where presumably it originated during or just before the First World War, it seems to have no other application than to get terrifically excited, especially without much cause. The notion, one judges, was that if one inadvertently stepped into a swimming pool at its deepest part one would momentarily become quite agitated until discovery was made that the water was no more than shoulder deep. But though we sometimes apply the same meaning to the expression in America, we also use it for other deeds. Chiefly, I think, we mean by it the great agitation of high dudgeon or roaring temper. When Johnny with his air rifle pings a neat hole in the windshield of the new car, granddaddy is likely to go off the deep end and whale the tar out of Johnny. And we use it in much weaker senses. Of one who is reckless, of one who has got into hot water, of one who has married, or of one who is dotty, we say that he has gone in at (or off) the deep end.

I'm from Missouri; you've got to show me

Colonel William D. Vandiver, representative in Congress from Missouri from 1897 to 1905, is often said to have originated this expression, though he never claimed that distinction, nor does the evidence bear it out. However, he did use it in the course of a jocular informal speech before The Five O'clock Club of Philadelphia in 1899. The preceding speaker, Congressman John A. T. Hull, of Iowa, had twitted Vandiver for being the only guest not in evening clothes. The fact was that neither guest, being on a naval inspection trip, had brought dress clothes, but Hull had somehow managed to obtain them. In Vandiver's reply, according to his own statement, as reported in Mencken's *Supplement Two: The American Language,* he said:

He tells you that the tailors, finding he was here without dress suit, made one for him in fifteen minutes. I have a different explanation: you heard him say he came here without one, and you see him now with one that doesn't fit him. The explanation is that he stole mine, and that's why you see him with one on and me without any. This story from Iowa doesn't go with me. I'm from Missouri, and you'll have to show me.

But Paul I. Wellman, in an article that first appeared in the Kansas City *Times* (reprinted July 11, 1941, in the St. Louis *Post-Dispatch*), reported other and earlier claims. One was that made by General Emmett Newton, who said that he had coined it when, as a boy, he had accompanied his father to a Knights Templar convention in Denver in 1892. Boylike he made a collection of badges. Another collecter said, "I'll bet I have a better collection." To which the young Newton replied, "I'm from Missouri; you'll have to show me."

Another report, made originally by W. M. Ledbetter in the St. Louis *Star* and quoted in *The Literary Digest,* January 28, 1922, was that the reporter had first heard the phrase in Denver in 1897 or 1898, and upon further investigation found that it—

had originated in the mining town of Leadville, Colorado, where a strike had been in progress for a long time, and a number of miners from the zinc and lead district of Southwest Missouri had been imported. . . . These Joplin miners were unfamiliar with [mining practice in Leadville]. . . . In fact, the pit bosses were constantly using the expression, "That man is from Missouri, you'll have to show him."

This report was later confirmed in a letter to the St. Louis *Post-Dispatch,* July 14, 1941, by Joseph P. Gazzam, who had been a mine superintendent in Leadville during that strike in 1896, and who had personally used the expression at the time.

But Wellman also reports a much earlier claim, made by Dr. Walter B. Stevens, author of *A Colonial History of Missouri* (1921):

. . . an officer of a Northern army [during the Civil War] fell upon a body of Confederate troops commanded by a Missourian. The Northerner demanded a surrender, saying he had so many thousand men in his command. The Confederate commander, game to the core, said he didn't believe the Northerner's boast of numerical superiority, and appended the now famous expression, "I'm from Missouri; you'll have to show me."

hell on wheels

Very tough, vicious, wild, or, especially of towns of the "wild and woolly West," lawless. During the construction of the Union Pacific Railroad back in the 1860's, as also on later western railroads, every temporary town successively at the end of the line—largely occupied by construction gangs living in boxcars, by liquor dealers, gamblers, and other "camp followers"—received the apt, though transient, name "Hell-on-wheels." As a result, any person or animal having vicious tendencies, especially a mule, or any vice-ridden, lawless town is said to be "hell on wheels." The expression is also applied derisively to men who pretend undeserved superiority.

to double in brass

To work in two jobs in order to increase one's income; to earn money from two sources; originally, and still, to play in the band as well as to perform. The expression is used primarily by theatrical people, especially by old-timers, when referring to an actor who, for economic reasons, appears as two different characters in a play. Undoubtedly, however, it originated in the circus, the American circus as developed by Phineas Taylor Barnum. And probably it was altogether literal in the early days of "The Greatest Show on Earth"—back, say, in the 1880's. Literal also in the one-ring circuses which hit the small towns today. The equestrian, the aerial trapeze artist, the clown who can also play a cornet, trombone, or clarinet in the street parade and when not engaged in his act has a better chance of employment than the straight musician or the straight performer. The expression, literal or figurative, seems to be unknown in England; at least it does not appear in the latest collections of British "unconventional English."

elbow grease

Just plain exercise for the elbows, or, rather, for the arms and elbows, such as scrubbing for the females of the species or polishing the car for the males. Elbow grease is the best kind of polish, it used to be said, to get furniture smooth and lustrous. The term was well known back in the seventeenth century, and was defined by a dictionary of slang at the end of that century—*A Dictionary of the Terms of the Canting Crew*—as, "A derisory Term for Sweat."

to be skinned out of one's eyeteeth

To be right royally hornswoggled, bamboozled or flimflammed, that is, cheated or deceived—and there are twenty or more less polite ways to express the unfair methods employed in such skulduggery. Whereas the expression "to cut one's eyeteeth" indicates that one has reached (presumably) years of discretion, "to have one's eyeteeth drawn"—or the American version, "to be skinned out of one's eyeteeth"—conveys the reverse impression, to be duped, to be made a fool. It is the hayseed taken over by city slickers or, conversely, the man or his wife coming from a big city to a country village who is most likely to be skinned out of his eyeteeth.

to tie the can to one

To give one the air; to fire, bounce, dismiss from employment; to expel. Although cans were in use a thousand years ago, this American slang could have had no meaning then, nor, for that matter, would we have recognized as cans the articles that then bore the name. Cans in those days, and for many centuries thereafter, were made of wood, or stone, or pottery. It was not until about the mid-eighteenth century that metal was introduced in the making. Today, though we still "can" things in glass or stoneware, we think of a can as always made of metal, usually tin. And it was the tin can that gave rise to our current expression. Before the S.P.C.A. became a great deterrent to such practices, it was considered a rare rowdy sport to win by blandishment the confidence of some stray dog, then, with a piece of string, to tie a tin can to its tail, with perhaps a small stone or two in the can. The released dog, at the first friendly wag of its tail, would be startled by the resulting rattle and go tearing down the street yelping in fright at the noise from the bounding can from which it could not escape. One to whom the can is tied is, thus, one whose presence is no longer desired. And "to can" a person is to dismiss him.

castle in the air (or in Spain)

Un château en Espagne has been the French expression since the fourteenth century, and as the Greeks and the Romans and the ancient Egyptians could build such marvelous yarns around the arrangement of stars in the constellations—Orion's belt, Cassiopeia's chair, the Great Bear (Ursa Major), and so on, and so on—it must be that they, too, had some equivalent for a castle in Spain or in the air. Sometimes the early Gallic dream site was *en Asie,* or sometime *en Albanie,* but always in some land or region where one could not conceivably acquire space for so impossible an edifice as a castle. We first adopted the translation, "a castle in Spain," which appears in *The Romaunt of the Rose* (*c.* 1400): "Thou shalt make castels thanne in Spayne, And dreme of Ioye [joy], alle but in vayne." Some dream architects of the sixteenth century began to design their structures for the skies or for the air, as we do today, and with a third site in Spain.

as queer (or tight) as Dick's hatband

Absurdly queer, or, as the case may be, inordinately tight. The "Dick" alluded to in this metaphor was Richard Cromwell, "Lord Protector" of England for a few months, September 1658 to May 1659. He had been nominated by his father, the powerful Oliver Cromwell, to succeed him in this high office, and was actually so proclaimed. But whereas the father had served, at least from the death of Charles I in 1649, as quasi-king of England, king in fact if not in name, Richard would gladly have accepted both title and crown, had not the army been hostile to such action and, indeed, to Richard, who was shortly dismissed from office. The crown was the "hatband" in the saying, which was deemed a "queer" adornment for the head of one so briefly in highest office, and too "tight" for him to have worn in safety. (Let me add, however, this account is not accepted by the *Oxford English Dictionary,* though no better substitute is offered.)

at daggers drawn

Ready for a fight or at the point of fighting; in a state of open hostilities. The dagger became a generally accepted part of the gentlemanly costume in the middle of the sixteenth century, and, naturally, with the means of reprisal so conveniently at hand, any insult, suggestion of an insult, or gesture or remark from which an insult might possibly be inferred became an occasion for the drawing of a weapon on the spot or for the more formal challenge to duel. The original expression was "at daggers drawing," implying readiness to draw one's weapon in defense or in maintaining one's honor. It is found in the translation (1540) by Jehan Palsgrave, *The Comedye of Acolastus,* a German story of the Prodigal Son: "We neuer mete togyther, but we be at daggers drawynge."

an also-ran

A loser in a contest; hence, an unsuccessful or insignificant person; a failure. The term originated on the American turf, applied to any horse failing to take a place among the winners or to a jockey riding such a horse. In political circles the term is applied to any unsuccessful candidate for office. The earliest literary example of the political use appears to have been in a headline in the Cincinnati *Enquirer* of February 6, 1904, which read: "George B. Cox— He Heads the List of Also Rans." Now, George B. Cox, saloonkeeper, was long the notorious political boss of Cincinnati; he determined who should be candidates for office, but never ran for any office himself. And there were no candidates for any office in February of 1904. So I wrote to the *Enquirer* for an explanation. Here is the answer to my query, printed in the issue of April 8, 1954:

On the above date under a heading: "Hoodoo Of the Race Horse" "Having A Horse Named After You Is Bad Luck." The Enquirer reprinted a New York *Sun* story about a horse that had been named "George B. Cox" after the famous boss of Cincinnati, evidently without his knowledge or consent.

Early in its career the horse had won a number of races and had captured the fancy of horse-players, especially Cincinnatians, and every time the horse went to post the home folks bet heavily on him. But they over-raced the old plater and he couldn't win a race.

Finally the notoriety that resulted from the continual losses of the horse became so derisive [as] to arouse the newspapers opposed to Boss Cox, and they seized on every loss during an election period to manufacture opprobrious slogans calling attention each time to such loss in page one headlines; while covering the election of Cox's candidates under a small head somewhere in the middle of the paper.

At what should have been the peak of its career, however, the horse disappeared from the tracks, but writers of the period reported a ringer as having been seen on several tracks in Ohio. Boss Cox had tried to get the owner of the horse to change its name. Whether he had succeeded or not was mere conjecture.

to cut capers

The sense, to anyone whose knowledge of Latin enables him to recognize that the zodiacal sign Capricorn is a he-goat, is to perform like a goat, especially a kid or young goat; that is, to frolic about in a grotesque manner. Although the expression and its meaning were still new in his day, Shakespeare introduces it in *Twelfth Night* (1601) in a dialog between the two cronies, Sir Toby Belch and Sir Andrew Aguecheek, Act I, scene 3:

Sir Andrew: I am a fellow o' the strangest mind i' the world; I delight in masques and revel sometimes altogether.
Sir Toby: Art thou good at these kickshaws, knight?
Sir Andrew: As any man in Illyria, whatsoever he be, under the degree of my betters; and yet I will not compare with an old man.
Sir Toby: What is thy excellence in a galliard [a lively French dance], knight?
Sir Andrew: Faith, I can cut a caper.
Sir Toby: And I can cut the mutton to it.

lead-pipe cinch

We borrowed "cinch" from the Spanish *cincha,* a saddle-girth, used by the early settlers of our present West and Southwest. And because the former girths of braided horsehair were so strong and could be drawn so tight that a rider could have no fear of a slipping saddle, "a cinch" became a synonym for a sure-fire certainty, something so assured that it could be considered easy. But why "lead pipe" was introduced into the phrase some fifty or sixty years ago has me mystified. An anonymous paragraph picked up a few years back says that a mythical cowboy, troubled by a bucking bronco that often snapped its cinch, throwing both saddle and rider, gave him the notion to make his cinch out of lead pipe. But as one who has had experience, not only with horses but also with lead pipe, I can imagine few materials more productive of uncertainty than the latter. Lead is far down the scale in tensile strength, and a cinch devised of lead pipe would be little more sturdy than cotton string.

ace in the hole

Something of especial effectiveness held in reserve or undisclosed; something kept up one's sleeve. The expression derives from the game of stud poker. In this game the first round of cards in each deal is dealt face down, and each such card remains undisclosed to all but its holder until the end of the hand. The next round is dealt face up, and that player with an exposed card of highest value may open the betting (or he may throw down his cards and pass the betting to the holder of the next best card). Bets may be called or raised, or a player may pass out, but when the bets are even among the remaining players the dealer deals the third round, also face up. Betting is resumed as before, the player with exposed cards of highest value having the privilege of opening. When betting is again even, the fourth round is dealt, again face up, and betting is again resumed as before. Upon the fifth and final round, also face up, each player then knows the full value of his own hand —his "hole card," the one undisclosed, plus the cards that have been exposed. After final bets are completed each player exposes his card "in the hole" and the best hand wins. Since aces are cards of highest value, that player with one, two, or three exposed aces and "an ace in the hole" has a card of especial effectiveness.

to get (or have) cold feet

This was discussed as an American expression in *A Hog on Ice*, and also so considered by the editors of *A Dictionary of Americanisms* (1951). But Kenneth McKenzie, professor emeritus of Italian at Princeton, has found a much older instance of its use.

In a letter to me after the publication of my earlier book he said: "This expression can hardly have originated in the 1890's, as you state, for it is found in Ben Jonson's *Volpone* (1605), where he refers to it as a 'Lombard Proverb.' Some years ago I published a short article on the subject, 'Ben Jonson's Lombard Proverb,' in *Modern Language Notes,* Vol XXVII (1912), p. 263. There seems to be no doubt that Jonson heard it used by some Italian friend."

The pertinent part of this article reads: "In the second act of the play, Volpone, disguised as a 'mountebank doctor,' explains to the crowd why he has fixed his bank in an obscure nook of the Piazza of St. Mark's instead of a more prominent place:

Let me tell you: I am not, as your Lombard proverb saith, cold on my feet; or content to part with my commodities at a cheaper rate than I am accustomed: look not for it.

In other words, he is not so 'hard up' as to be obliged to sell his wares at a sacrifice."

Professor McKenzie's article goes on to relate that the proverb— *Avegh minga frecc i pee,* to have cold feet—is still used in Lombardy, with the figurative meaning, "to be without money." "And if a card player, as a pretext for quitting the game in which he has lost money, says that his feet are cold, the expression might come to mean in general 'to recede from a difficult position,' or more specifically, 'to have cold feet.' "

playing horse with a billy goat

Of course, "playing horse" is a childhood pastime—playing as if riding upon a horse. And "playing horse with (a person)" is indulging in horseplay—taking advantage of, or picking on, or joshing a person. But neither of these expresses the sense of the phrase used by my father and which my children and grandchildren understand, even when abbreviated into "pee-ing h. with a b. g." Others of my father's generation in central Ohio also knew its meaning, though I have not heard it elsewhere. As used by the cognoscente it conveys "engaging in something of uncertain outcome; or, making something or doing something which, for the present at least, is secret." Probably the billy goat was dragged into the picture just because it used to be fashionable among families of the less wealthy, who could not afford pony carts drawn by real ponies for their children, to have the carts but to substitute a billy goat or two for the ponies and thus more or less keep up with the Joneses.

codfish aristocracy

He didn't coin the term, but Wallace Irwin neatly expressed its meaning in the first stanza of "Codfish Aristocracy," which he has given me permission to quote:

> Of all the fish that swim or swish
> In ocean's deep autocracy,
> There's none possess such haughtiness
> As the codfish aristocracy.

In fact, the name was coined thirty years or more before Irwin was born in 1876. It originated in Massachusetts to denote a class of *nouveau riche* who had acquired wealth from the codfishing industry. George Stimpson in *A Book about a Thousand Things* (1946) reminds us that John Rowe, a Boston merchant, made a motion in the legislature on March 17, 1784, that "leave be given to hang up the representation of a Codfish in the room where the House sits, as a memorial of the importance of the Cod-Fishery to the welfare of the Commonwealth," a motion that was carried, thus accounting for the painted wooden codfish still hanging in the chamber of the House of Representatives in Massachusetts.

Mrs. Grundy

Do you picture her as a hoity-toity person, nose in air, prim, precise, lips pursed as if always saying "prunes" and "prisms"? Well, actually you may paint your own picture, for the dear lady never existed. She was an imaginary person in a play, a character frequently referred to but never appearing. The play was Thomas Morton's *Speed the Plough* (1798). Dame Ashby, one of the characters, is constantly on edge, fearing that some occasion may arise that will provoke the scorn of her neighbor, Mrs. Grundy, apparently the supreme exemplar of perfect propriety. "What will

Mrs. Grundy say?" is so often on the lips of the good dame that, thanks to the popularity of the comedy on both sides of the Atlantic, it became proverbial. Thus, in the second act speaking of her daughter, she says to her husband, "If shame should come to the poor child—I say, Tummus, what would Mrs. Grundy say then?" "Dom Mrs. Grundy," replies Farmer Ashby; "what wou'd my poor wold Heart zay?"

The line inspired the poet Frederick Locker-Lampson, in "The Jester," 1857, to write:

> It is an ugly world. Offend
> Good people, how they wrangle,
> The manner that they never mend,
> The characters they mangle.
> They eat, and drink, and scheme, and plod,
> And go to church on Sunday—
> And many are afraid of God—
> And more of Mrs. Grundy.

to put (or have) one's nose out of joint

To supplant one in the affection or esteem of another; hence, to humiliate; also, to upset one's plans. Usually it is the arrival of a baby in the family nowadays that puts the nose of a slightly older brother or sister, hitherto greatly favored, out of joint. But it can be, and formerly generally was, an older person. A parson or priest can have his nose put quite out of joint in his congregation by a substitute acting in his absence. And so can a doctor when a younger practictioner hangs up his shingle. And on up or down the line. In earliest usage the intent of the phrase was that of upsetting one's plans, and that was what was meant by Barnaby Rich in *His Farewell to Militarie Profession* (1581): "It could bee no other then his owne manne, that has thrust his nose so farre out of ioynte." The present prevailing interpretation, however, had been reached by 1662 when the diarist Samuel Pepys had apparently become addicted to the use of the expression. At least it occurs twice in his diary, each time, curiously, referring to the mistress of Charles II. The first entry, May 31st of that year reads:

. . . all people say of her [the king's recent bride, Catherine of Braganza] to be a very fine and handsome lady, and very discreet; and that the king is pleased enough with her; which, I fear, will put Madam Castlemaine's nose out of joynt.

The second, July 22nd, 1663, is:

He [Lord Sandwich] believes that, as soon as the King can get a husband for Mrs. Stewart, however, my Lady Castlemaine's nose will be out of joynt; for that she comes to be in great esteem, and is more handsome than she.

to keep one's shirt on

Perhaps because the shirts of a hundred years ago were not Sanforized and, therefore, the American male was likely to be hampered in the free movement of his arms, it was his custom, whenever a fight seemed imminent in settling an argument, to remove his

shirt first, and thus be ready to wade in with both fists flailing. The opponent, however, might see that there were two sides to the matter under debate; therefore, that it would not be necessary to resort to fisticuffs. Accordingly, his admonition would be, "Now, just keep your shirt on." At least, such is still the meaning—avoid becoming excited or angry; keep calm, cool, and collected—and was

when George W. Harris in *The Spirit of the Times* (1854) wrote, "I say, you durned ash cats, just keep yer shirts on, will ye?"

a tin-horn gambler (or sport)

We have to go back to the times of the Gold Rush of the Far West for the original specimen, and the people who used the term then thought they were giving a literal name to the person or persons who were thus described. In other words, the name was applied to those gamblers who could not take the chances of the more aristocratic and costly game of faro, and were obliged to content themselves with the less pretentious game of chuck-a-luck. This is a game played with three dice, the gamblers betting the house that (a) all three will turn up with the same number, or (b) that the sum of the three will equal a certain number, or (c) that at least one of the three will appear with a specified number on its face. To relieve the monotony of shaking the dice all evening long the operators employed "a small churn-like affair" which, popularly, was called a tin horn. The game was a cheap one and, in consequence, the would-be sports who played it became tin-horn gamblers or sports, a term nowadays applied to anyone making a flashy appearance on a cheap scale.

to hang by a thread

To be subject to imminent danger; to be in a hazardous position or precarious condition. The allusion is to one Damocles, a courtier in the reign of Dionysius of Syracuse in the fifth century B.C. All we know of this courtier is from the tale told both by Cicero and by Horace. He was given to extreme flattery of his ruler, and, one day, having praised extravagantly the power of Dionysius was invited to see for himself just how much happiness that power brought. Accordingly he was given a magnificent feast, and was surrounded by luxury and entertainment beyond description. In the midst of this, however, he happened to glance above him and saw, suspended by a single hair, a naked sword pointed directly over his head. The intent, of course, was to show that a king, perhaps even more than his subjects, could never enjoy unalloyed happiness. We also refer to the *sword of Damocles* as a symbol of impending doom or threat of danger.

badger game

A form of blackmail, employed upon a man of position or wealth who is enticed into a compromising situation by a woman and is then "discovered" by one professing to be her husband. To avoid disgrace under threat of legal procedure or newspaper publicity the victim is under the thumb of the conniving operators. To badger, in criminal slang, is to blackmail. This meaning arose from the cruel sport of badger baiting, practiced from time immemorial until comparatively recent years, in which a live badger was placed in an artificial hole, such as a barrel, and dogs were set upon it. Thus "to badger" came to mean "to worry, tease, pester," or, leading to the sense above, "to subject a person in one's power to persecution; hence, to blackmail." This form of blackmail is probably as old as the hills, but association with the term "badger" and the present name of the practice are American innovations of the past hundred years.

ambulance chaser

Derogatory term for a lawyer who, after an accident, immediately seeks the person injured and, for a contingent fee, offers his professional services in a suit for damages. This profession of dubious ethics, or at least the descriptive term, apparently originated in New York City in the 1890's, during the period when the notorious partnership of criminal lawyers, Howe & Hummel, was entering the height of its career.

alpha and omega

The first and the last; the beginning and the end. Both the expression itself—the first and the last letters of the Greek alphabet—and its definition are from the Bible, The Revelation of St. John the Divine. The phrase is repeated four times—in the eighth and eleventh verses of the first chapter, in the sixth verse of the twenty-first chapter, and in the thirteenth verse of the twenty-second chapter.

hammer and tongs

With all the vigor at one's command; forcefully; with might and main. Usually one goes after another hammer and tongs; that is, with no holds barred; with every intent to take him apart literally or figuratively. But on the domestic scene, a wife may go after the spouse, or the reverse, hammer and tongs, orally flaying him or her, or perhaps even hurling crockery or other solid articles. The allusion is to the old-time blacksmith who, with his tongs, long-handled pincers, took a piece of red-hot metal from the forge, laid it upon his anvil and beat it into shape with his hammer. Nowadays the blacksmith with his forge, his hammer, and his tongs has just about disappeared from the scene; his art is being replaced by insensate machinery, but the language of his trade will long remain.

sailing under false colors

Assuming to be what one is not; being a pretender or hypocrite. This arose from the days of piracy on the high seas, when a pirate vessel, sighting a possible prey, hoisted the flag of a friendly nation to its halyards to allay suspicion while it drew within striking distance, thus catching the unsuspecting victim unprepared for defense. But "under false colors" was in earlier use in a similar sense, denoting a man, sect, or even an army appearing in the garb or under the badge or insignia of a house or party of which he was not a member. From this were derived such phrases as "to come out in one's true colors" and "to show one's colors"; that is, to reveal one's true nature or standing.

to cry over spilt milk

To grieve over that which is irretrievably lost or beyond recovery; to regret that which has been said or done. Though the actual occurrence, with high milk prices, is something over which housewives probably have wept—or over a torn fig leaf—since the time of Eve, they never think of the ones benefiting from the accident—the dog, the cat, or the milkman—just their own selfish loss. The first to give voice to this cold comfort in this manner, in print at least, was that prime humorist of the past century, Thomas C. Haliburton. In his first series of *The Clockmaker; or the Sayings and Doings of Samuel Slick of Slickville* (1836), a friend says, "What's done, Sam, can't be helped, there is no use in cryin over spilt milk."

to get one's goat

To bewilder, confuse, or baffle; to irritate, annoy, or vex; to fuss one; to make one nervous; to get under one's skin (as said of the chigger); to give one a pain in the neck. Efforts have been made to trace this American expression back to a Greek source, but without conspicuous success. The French, however, do have an expression, *prendre la chèvre*, which, though defined, "to take offense," has the literal meaning, "to take, or to snatch, the goat." Their expression is said to have appeared as early as the sixteenth century, and does appear in seventeenth century as well as current dictionaries. Nevertheless it is most probable that American usage, traceable only to the early twentieth century, was of independent origin: first, because the French phrase does not have the same literal meaning, and, second, even if it did, the borrowing and literal translation would have been much earlier. One account weakly explains our phrase as derived from the racing stable where, sometimes, a goat browses among the horses on the theory that it has a calming effect upon high-strung racers. Deliberate borrowing of the goat from such a stable might thus be considered an unfriendly act, according to that explanation. Be that as it may, the earliest literary quotation thus far exhumed appears in Jack London's *Smoke Bellew* (1912), Chapter VII, "The Little Man," in which the usage has nothing to do with horse-racing. Here "Smoke" and "the little man" face the danger of crossing a rotting snow-bridge over a crevasse. "The little man" crosses first and waits for "Smoke." " 'Your turn,' he called across. 'But just keep a-coming and don't look down. That's what got my goat. Just keep a-coming, that's all. And get a move on. It's almighty rotten.' "

six of one and half a dozen of the other

No choice; one and the same; even steven. There seems to have been no specific allusion involved in this expression, nothing beyond the fact that half a dozen is six. It first appeared in Marryat's *The Pirate and the Three Cutters* (1836). Several of the sailors, repairing the ravages of a storm, have fallen to talking about some of the passengers, especially about the black nurse of white twins on board. Jack says to Bill, "You've been sweet on that . . . girl for these last three weeks." "Any port in a storm," Bill replies, "but she won't do for harbor duty—it's the babies I likes." At which Jack jeers, "I knows the women, but I never knows the children. It's just six of one and half-a-dozen of the other, ain't it, Bill?"

(big) butter-and-egg man

Derisive term for one of the *nouveau riche,* for one ostentatiously displaying new wealth. The expression came into popularity about 1925, during the Coolidge regime of almost hectic national prosperity, when office workers and mill hands alike were sporting silk shirts. Everyone was playing the stock market and reaping enormous paper profits. A large army of short-lived millionaires was the result, many of whom, not to the manner born, threw their new-found money around in wild splurges, especially on chorus girls. Unlike the older and more respected "captains of industry," these men sought control of no big business, such as railroads, or mines, or motorcars. Lacking a specific appellation for such a spender, New York columnists dubbed him a "butter-and-egg man," taking the term from the title of a play by George Kaufman produced in 1925.

deus ex machina (a god from a machine)

This Latin phrase really refers to a stage effect in Greek plays. That is to say, Greek tragic playwrights frequently introduced one or another of the gods for the purpose of explaining some situation or solving some difficulty. Representing gods, the characters who played the parts could not walk out upon the stage as did other players, but were let down upon the stage from above by the aid of a mechanical device constructed for the purpose. Such was a god from a machine, *deus ex machina,* one who appeared suddenly and unexpectedly, ready to solve any difficulty.

to pay the fiddler (or piper)

To bear the consequences; suffer the penalties; defray the costs. The first is the American version and "to pay the piper" is the English. Fiddles furnished the music for stately English ballrooms, but flutes or pipes were the conventional music for English rustic dances, whereas the country dances of America relied on fiddles. In its figurative sense the English phrase dates back to Thomas Flatman's *Heraclitus ridens* (1681): "After all this Dance he has led the Nation, he must at least come to pay the Piper himself." The American phrase is very probably much older than the first citation shown in *The Dictionary of Americanisms* which quotes John Edwards' *Shelby and His Men* (1867): "Those who dance must pay the fiddler, says an adage." The incongruity is that the proverbial "fiddler's pay," even in England, was nothing more than thanks and all the wine he could drink, hence the metaphor, "drunk as a fiddler."

to shoot the bull (bull session)

Back in my college days a "bull session" was a gathering of young men—always men and always young—congregated informally in some dormitory room over late coffee or beer or other refreshments, with conversation ranging over any topic or topics that might be argued or discussed. The topics might be religion, giving rise to a diversity of views or half-formed ideas, or sex, or music, art, literature, or anything discussable, but none of the participants in such a session certainly ever considered these sessions—sometimes, though rarely, including a college prof or instructor—to consist of "foolish talk, stuff, claptrap," in the words of a recent dictionary. The discussants took them seriously, no matter what others may have thought—though, of course, frivolity did enter now and then. But along about that time "bull" degenerated into another sense, euphemistically often called "bushwa," what one might describe as the end product of the domestic bull, used chiefly as fertilizer; its slang sense was idle talk, stuff, nonsense, claptrap. The "bull session" of earlier days then descended into any confabulation, male or female, devoted to such chatter, and "to shoot the bull" did then become hyperbole for "to talk nonsense" or, sometimes, "to brag," or "to cheat or defraud."

Anthony (or Antony) over

The great collector of Americanisms, Schele De Vere, calls this an American game and defines it (1872): "A game of ball played by two parties of boys, on opposite sides of a schoolhouse, over which the ball is thrown." He localizes it in Pennsylvania, but it was also played in southern Ohio in my boyhood, and, if I recall correctly, also in my later youth in the suburbs of New York City. But why the game carries the name Anthony (or Antony) is a mystery. Possibly the reference was to St. Anthony who, upon appeal, is credited with aid in finding lost objects, as it was always an object by either of the "two parties of boys" to so throw the ball as to go far over the heads of the opposing party, perhaps to be lost in high grass or weeds.

as dead as the dodo

Utterly extinct; obsolete; completely washed up. The reference is to a peculiar flightless bird of which only two species were known, those found respectively on the islands of Mauritius and Réunion, lying east of Madagascar. The birds, as described by voyagers to  the islands in the sixteenth and seventeenth centuries, were larger than the swan and with much heavier bodies. Being slow of motion and unable, with their small wings, to fly, they were easily killed by voyagers and early settlers, who found them highly edible, and especially by the pigs introduced to the islands by colonists. Before the end of the seventeenth century the species on Mauritius had all been exterminated; a few still remained on Réunion into the early eighteenth century before complete extermination. As Will Cuppy said in *How to Become Extinct* (1941), "The Dodo never had a chance. He seems to have been invented for the sole purpose of becoming extinct and that was all he was good for."

to take a back seat

To take a seat or occupy a position among those of little importance; to practice humility or become humble; to go 'way back and sit down. There's little doubt that this expression was an outcome of the natural characteristics of Americans. The aggressive, those determined to be heard on any subject up for discussion, inevitably plant themselves toward the front of any assembly, so that they may rise and be seen readily by those whom they wish to persuade. The humble, those who instinctively avoid the limelight, as well as those who hide their lights under a bushel, willingly keep in the background. A back-seat driver, however, is a horse of another color. He—or usually she—knows not the meaning of the word "humility." On the contrary, she is the aggressive one, dictating from the rear seat what the actual driver in the front seat, usually her husband, should do, what road he should take, how slow he should drive, what he should do in any emergency, and so on.

to cut the mustard

To accomplish, be able to, or succeed with; to meet expectations; to play, as music, expertly. To get at the origin of this altogether American expression we have to go back to the beginning of the century when "to be the proper mustard" was a slang phrase meaning to be the genuine article, possibly because some so-called "mustard" of that period would not pass today's pure food requirements. From that, immediately, came "all to the mustard," that is, all one could ask for, fine and dandy, "copesetic," as the late Bill Robinson would say. Then hotly, as early as 1907, came our present phrase. O. Henry used it in *Heart of the West* in that year: "I looked around and found a proposition that exactly cut the mustard." It's just a slang expression, bearing no connection to the use of the verb "cut" in the sense of to reduce the strength of.

to bury the hatchet

To settle differences and take up friendly relations. In *A Hog on Ice* I made the statement that, although we are accustomed to connect this expression with practices of the American Indian, I had not been able to find that there was any such ritual or saying among the tribes of North America. Accordingly I considered it a variation of the fourteenth-century English saying, "to hang up the hatchet," of similar meaning.

Mitford M. Mathews, in an article in *American Speech* (May, 1953), indicates unmistakably that I did not delve as deeply as I should have into the customs of the American Indian. He quotes, as the earliest record, this statement, dated 1680, from the writings of Samuel Sewall: "Meeting with the Sachem they came to an agreement and buried two Axes in the ground; . . . which ceremony to them is more significant and binding than all Articles of Peace the Hatchet being a principal weapon." *The Dictionary of Americanisms* (1951), edited by Dr. Mathews, carries further evidence confuting my statement. Thus, under *tomahawk*, is a quotation from Robert Beverley's *The History and Present State of Virginia* (1705): "They use . . . very ceremonious ways in concluding of Peace . . . such as burying a Tomahawk." Other quotations from those dates onward, under both *hatchet* and *tomahawk,* demonstrate that the custom was well established, as was also the custom of "taking up the hatchet" when warlike activities began.

raining cats and dogs

Dean Jonathan Swift has been given credit for originating this extravagant way of indicating excessive or torrential rain, but I doubt that he did. To be sure its first literary appearance in this

form is in his *Polite Conversation* (1783), but it must not be forgotten that these so-called "dialogues" are markedly satirical, and when he has Lord Sparkish say, "I know Sir John will go, though he was sure it would rain cats and dogs; but pray stay, Sir John," he is using what he regards as a hackneyed phrase, as he does deliberately throughout these dialogues. The hyperbole was probably more than a hundred years old by that time. As evidence, go back to Richard Brome's play *The City Witt* (*c.* 1652). In Act IV, scene 1, we find Sarpego—the pedant who, affecting a great knowledge of Latin, translates it entirely by ear—speaking: "From henceforth *Erit fluvius Deucalionis*/The world shall flow with dunces; *Regna bitque*/and it shall rain; *Dogmata Polla Sophon*/Dogs and Polecats, and so forth."

to eat one's hat

To eat crow; to eat humble pie; to assert one's readiness to consume such an unsavory mess if a certain event should not turn out as one predicts. The present form of the saying is first found in

184 ·

Charles Dickens' *Pickwick Papers* (1837): " 'If I knew as little of life as that, I'd eat my hat and swallow the buckle whole.' " Dickens could have coined the phrase, but it is more likely that it was merely his own adaptation of the older, "I'll eat old Rowley's hat," of the same general significance. Here "old Rowley" referred to Charles II, a nickname given to him, it is said, from his favorite race horse, but cherished by his adherents from the long struggle against Oliver Cromwell, through punning connection with the familiar saying, "a Rowley [Roland] for an Oliver."

to row (someone) up Salt river

To defeat, overcome, vanquish an adversary; especially, politically, to defeat an opposing candidate in an election. For many years the expression was used only in the latter sense, based on an alleged incident. The story, gravely cited by the recent *Dictionary of American History* on the authority of various earlier accounts, takes it back to the presidential campaign of 1832, when the Whig candidate, Henry Clay, was running against Andrew Jackson. Clay on a Western speaking trip, it was said, hired a boatman to take him up the Ohio river to Louisville, but the boatman, a Jackson supporter, took him up Salt river instead, causing Clay to miss his engagement by several hours. Clay's defeat was assumed to have hinged on that episode; hence, the political application of the phrase.

That story was accepted as the origin of the expression for more than a hundred years. Apparently it did not occur to anyone to doubt that Henry Clay, who had lived in Lexington, Kentucky, from the time he was twenty, could have been bamboozled into an acceptance of the comparatively narrow Salt river for the broad expanse of the Ohio, or that Louisville had suddenly been moved some thirty miles downstream. It was not until recently that doubt was thrown upon the accepted version.

The skeptics were Professor Hans Sperber of Ohio State University and Professor James N. Tidwell of San Diego State College. As they report in *American Speech* (December, 1951), the expression antedated the Clay-Jackson campaign by at least several years. Salt river was already notorious as the seat of Western tall talk among rivermen; it was the home of the "ring-tailed roarer or screamer of the half-horse, half-alligator breed," of backwoods braggarts or rowdies who would make life miserable for a stranger. Their conclusion: "*To row up Salt River* and *to row somebody up Salt River* as used in actual or fictional backwoods slang mean, respectively, to be engaged in a difficult or probably unsuccessful journey and to make somebody undergo hardships or, more particularly, to give him a beating. The corresponding political phrases are nothing but natural applications of these meanings to political conditions."

On my own, I surmise that the original speakers intended to "roar" a person up Salt river by their outrageously exaggerated tall talk; in their speech "roar" became "ro'," which the listener interpreted to be "row."

to draw the line

To reach one's limit; especially, to fix a definite limit of procedure beyond which one refuses to go. Although now figurative, the line that was drawn was originally actual. It was the cut of a plowshare across the field to indicate the limit of one's holding, back in the sixteenth century.

try it on the dog

To experiment on (someone or something); to try out the effects of something upon someone. In all probability, though proof is lacking, this was a literal test originally—experimentation, probably with meat, possibly tainted, or with some other doubtful food upon the household dog to determine alimental effect upon the human system. The idea, at least, traces back to the official taster in days when royalty was always fearful of being poisoned by a cook secretly employed by an envious brother or cousin. However, our present expression came into theatrical usage around the latter quarter of the nineteenth century, when, first in England, the producers of a new play sometimes decided to "try it out on the dog," meaning to test the reaction of some provincial or matinee audience and thus be able to correct any faults before introducing the play in London. In America, a play is "tried out on the dog" by being first played in Hartford, New Haven, Philadelphia, or perhaps Boston, before it appears on Broadway. But the expression is applied now quite generally; almost any new product is first tested upon a limited number of "dogs" before it is placed on general sale.

up Salt Creek (without a paddle)

In a pretty kettle of fish; behind the 8-ball; on the spot; in a predicament. Salt Creek is not the same body of water as Salt river (q.v.), up which a political party or candidate is sometimes rowed, or at least its political allusion is different. In fact, since one who is up this creek is often also said to be "without a paddle," the inference is that it was originally an actual salt-water indentation from the sea, a passageway through marshland, from which egress would be extremely difficult without proper means of locomotion. The American expression is at least seventy years old, having been used in a campaign song of 1884 called "Blaine up Salt Creek."

poor as a church mouse

Mighty poor; about as deprived of the necessities of life as the "fly on the wall" of which my wife used to recite lugubriously to the children:

> Poor little fly on the wall,
> Ain't got no shimmy-shirt,
> Ain't got no pettiskirt,
> Ain't got no nothing at all!
> Poor little fly on the wall.

But our church mouse is not found only in English-speaking countries. The Germans have the same saying, *arm wie eine Kirchenmaus;* in French it's *gueux comme un rat d'église,* and it is found also in other languages. The English saying goes back to the seventeenth century, but was probably taken over from French. It is likely that it arose from some folk tale relating the sad experience of a mouse trying to find food for itself and its starving little ones in a church. No pantry, no meal bag, no grain bin made the struggle for existence most difficult.

to set one's cap at (or for) a person

To strive to gain the affection of a person: always said of a woman or maiden who, perhaps modestly or perhaps ostentatiously, puts her best foot forward in her efforts to gain the attention and win the admiration of the male she favors as a lifelong companion in matrimony. The expression was once more literal than figurative. Back in the days when women considered a light muslin cap a necessary part of ordinary indoor attire, it was but natural for a maiden, a spinster, or a widow to don her most becoming or fanciest cap when an eligible swain came to call. Of course young brother or nephew Diccon would spot the dress-up headgear, and the family would adopt his remark that Molly or Aunty Prue was "setting her cap at" the young squire or the parson. The common expression may go back to the seventeenth century, but was certainly known to Oliver Goldsmith in the eighteenth. The younger generation of today probably does not know it.

a pain in the neck

Not an actual physical pain, nor is it located so much in the neck as in the head. That is, the pain is mental, rather than physical. One who is the cause, who is the pain or gives the pain, is just *persona non grata* to the recipient. Others may consider him or her a pleasant and entertaining person, even well informed, but to the sufferer he or she is an unmitigated bore. The cause of the pain may also be inanimate; that is, a house or a picture or a newspaper, or anything which one regards as contemptible or lacking in merit. The expression is American slang of the past fifty years, a polite variation of a pain previously associated with another part of the anatomy.

not to know B from a battledore (or broomstick, or from a bull's foot, or buffalo's foot)

To know not one letter from another; not to know beans; to be wholly illiterate, or extremely ignorant. This accusation of complete illiteracy dates at least to the late Middle English period, according to *The Rolls Series* (the chronicles and memorials of Great Britain during the Middle Ages). The earlier expression, perhaps originating in an agricultural section, seems to have been that comparing B to the foot of a bull, but by the time of John Foxe's *Actes and Monuments of these Latter and Perilous Dayes* (1563) the more courtly battledore was the fashionable term: "He knew not a B from a battledore nor even a letter of the book." Broomstick and the American buffalo's foot were later variations, the latter first appearing in James K. Paulding's *Westward Ho!* (1832). Mere alliteration, not real or fancied resemblance, seems to have been the only motive back of any of the comparisons, just as in the antonym, "to know a hawk from a handsaw," indicative of intelligence.

iron curtain

This expression, in its allusion to the line across Europe beyond which are the countries under Soviet influence or control, was credited, in *A Hog on Ice,* to Winston Churchill, to its use in a speech delivered by him on March 5, 1946, at Westminster College, Fulton, Missouri. But the same metaphor may have been in other minds also and was certainly used by others before that date. Had the idea of an impenetrable curtain occurred to an American, it is likely that he would have called it "an asbestos curtain," having in mind the curtains used in American theaters to stop a backstage fire from spreading to the audience. But in Europe such fireproof curtains have long been made of iron.

Thus, some five months before Churchill's speech, there was an article in the *Sunday Empire News* (London), October 21, 1945, with the heading, "An Iron Curtain across Europe," describing the difficulties attending military government in Germany. It was written by a former staff officer in the G_5 Division of SHAEF, Sir St. Vincent Troubridge, who is also familiar with theatrical terms and expressions. In a letter to me he stated that the expression immediately caught the fancy of the London newspaper world and within a month or two appeared in leading articles and that it was used at least once in the House of Commons before Churchill gave it world-wide circulation.

However, though without doubt unknown to either Troubridge or Churchill, the same metaphorical application had been given to the expression eight months earlier by no less a person than Joseph Goebbels, German Propaganda Chief. As reported by John A. Lukacs in *The Great Powers & Eastern Europe,* 1953, Goebbels wrote in his editorial of February 23, 1945, in *Das Reich*:

If the German people should lay down their arms, the agreement between Roosevelt, Churchill and Stalin would allow the Soviets to occupy all Eastern and South-Eastern Europe, together with the major part of the Reich. An iron curtain [*eiserner Vorhang*] would at once descend on this territory, which, including the Soviet Union, would be of tremendous dimension. . . .

Goebbels was a good prophet.

To forestall the critics, let me add that other metaphorical applications of *iron curtain,* though not to the Soviets, may be found in the story, "The Food of the Gods," by H. G. Wells (1904), with reference to a person held incommunicado by the police; in a book, *A Mechanistic View of War and Peace* (1915), by George Crile, and in *England, Their England* (1933), by A. G. MacDonnell, each of the latter two with reference to a curtain of artillery fire in a military engagement.

to bite the thumb at

"I will bite my thumb at them; which is a disgrace to them, if they bear it," said Sampson of the house of Capulet to his fellow servant, Gregory, in Act I, scene 1, of *Romeo and Juliet.* But a moment later, when it appeared that the servants of the house of Montague were not going to "bear it," he amended the remark: "No, sir, I do not bite my thumb at you, sir, but I bite my thumb, sir."

That is, to bite one's thumb was, and still is, an ordinary act, as ordinary and inoffensive as to bite one's fingernail. But "to bite one's thumb at" a person was an insult of Shakespeare's time not to be taken lightly, a sure cause for quarrel. The gesture itself, as defined by Cotgrave (1611), meant, "to threaten or defie by putting the thumbe naile into the mouth, and with a ierke [from the upper teeth] make it to knack [click, snap]." But the commentators of Shakespeare and others have not been able to determine the significance of the gesture, what it was intended to represent. The conjecture is that it was equivalent to the indecent gesture of contempt, the thumb thrust between the fingers to represent a fig (see under "not worth a fig" in *A Hog on Ice,* p. 125), but it is difficult to see what relationship there could have been between the two.

tied to one's mother's (or wife's) apron strings

Apparently this whole idea of domination by one's mother—more rarely, wife nowadays—arose from a law going back at least three hundred years under which a man might have a tenure of property only by virtue of his wife, sometimes only through her  lifetime. That tenure was known as an "apron-string hold." The wife, obviously, controlled the finances of the family and, undoubtedly, frequently wore the pants. At least it was easy to extend the sense of the figure and to have the husband tied to his wife's apron strings, as Thomas Macaulay put it in his *History of England* (1849). But by that time also that which worked so successfully with papa was carried on by mama to such others of her family as might be benefited. Little Bud, who had looked to mama to wipe his nose as a child, continued to look to her through adolescence and even into adulthood. Perhaps the only blessing from a war is that it enables many young men to become untied from mother's apron strings.

to put the bite on one

To mooch, cadge, shake down, or, more plainly, to beg. This American slang seems to have developed from the entirely innocent token of fondness, "to bite one's ear." In *Romeo and Juliet,* Mercutio makes reply to a quip from Romeo, his dearest friend, "I will bite thee by the eare for that iest." The expression, though perhaps not the action, originated from the French, *mordre l'oreille,* a soft caress and whispered endearment accompanied by a gentle nip of the ear. Now, in making a request for a loan or in begging, one does not shout from the housetops, but if possible one whispers his wants in the ear of the intended victim. He is "putting the bite on," though from appearances he is but "biting a friend by the ear."

busman's holiday

Spare time spent in doing the same thing one does in one's regular occupation. The story is that the regular driver of a London bus actually did that—spent one of his days off riding as a passenger alongside the driver who was taking his place. But if that episode ever occurred, no report of it has yet been found. The age of the expression cannot be determined, but it had become proverbial many years before the first reported appearance in print—1921. A carpenter who, on a holiday repairs his own porch—a schoolteacher who uses his weekends as a Boy Scout master—a newspaper reporter who, at night, writes fiction; each may be said to take a busman's holiday.

drawing a longbow

One who numbers golfers or fishermen among his acquaintances should quickly recognize the nature of this expression. Any tale which in the telling makes use of unusual distance or unusual size that cannot be subjected to verification is very likely to be stretched in the telling. Thus it was even in the days of Robin Hood. For two hundred years—roughly between 1300 and 1500—the might of England rested on its archers. The kings, from Edward II to Henry VIII, in all ways encouraged an increase in this skill; in fact, successively they commanded the general practice of archery on holidays and Sundays, to the exclusion of all other pastimes. The weapon was the longbow (now often written "long bow"), a bow distinguished from the common bow in being not less than five feet in length, and sometimes specified as being one foot taller than the archer. Both skill and strength were required to draw such bows, but prodigious feats of skill and strength were shown by the bowmen—if one were credulous enough to accept the tales of the mighty archer or his friends. Outdoing the exploits of William Tell, an old English ballad recites the deed of an archer who, shooting before the king, split a thin wand in two at a distance of a quarter of a mile (!), then in further proof of skill he sent his arrow through an apple placed on the head of his young son at a distance of 120 yards. And Robin Hood and the valiant Little John, 'twas said, could place an arrow a measured mile. 'Tis plain why our expression has long meant stretching the truth; exaggerating; telling a tall tale.

Cadmean victory

A victory in which the victor has suffered such great loss as hardly to be distinguished from the vanquished. The term derives from the mythological founding of Thebes. Cadmus, prince of Phenicia, searching for his lost sister, was advised by an oracle to abandon the search and to follow a cow and establish a city where she should lie down. The cow led him into Bœotia where, before Cadmus could carry out the charge to found a city, his companions were all devoured by a dragon. Cadmus thereupon slew the dragon and, at the command of the goddess Athene, scattered its teeth over the field. Immediately armed men sprang from the teeth and fiercely turned upon the hero. To divert the threat, however, Cadmus induced them to turn upon each other. When all but five were thus slain, Cadmus stopped the strange duel and persuaded the five to assist him in the founding of the city. Hence also the expression, *to sow dragon's teeth,* meaning, to sow seeds of strife and discord.

to take the bark off

To tan; give one a hiding; to lambaste, or, in simpler speech, to flog, chastise. Possibly the original idea, likening the bark of a tree to the skin of a man, was to castigate, to flog as with a cat-o'-nine-tails, or, that is, to whip so severely as literally to flay the skin from one's back.

As easily imagined, "to take the bark off one" gives greater pain than "to talk the bark off a tree," though both are severe. The first is entirely physical, both literally and figuratively. The second is entirely figurative. The implication is that the one who does the talking gives such a tongue-lashing, or uses such cutting remarks as to resemble in effectiveness the strippers used in removing bark from a tree. Both expressions are homely American, probably dating back to the days of peeled logs for frontier cabins and strict disciplinary parents. Literary records as far as traced, however, do not show great antiquity—the first to 1845, and the second only to 1891.

to kill the fatted calf

To prepare for a season of rejoicing; to prepare a warm welcome. The allusion is to the parable of the prodigal son, Luke xv, verses 11 to 32, the younger son who took his portion of his patrimony and journeyed "into a far country, and there wasted his substance with riotous living. And when he had spent all, there arose a mighty famine in that land; and he began to be in want." Then, employed as a swineherd, "he would fain have filled his belly with the husks that the swine did eat." Finally, coming to his senses, he decided to return home, knowing that his father would at least give him better employment. "But when he was yet a great way off, his father saw him, and had compassion, and . . . said to his servants, Bring forth the best robe, and put it on him; and put a ring on his hand, and shoes on his feet: And bring hither the fatted calf, and kill it; and let us eat, and be merry: For this my son was dead, and is alive again; he was lost, and is found. And they began to be merry."

in cahoots with (one)

In close coöperation with; in league with; in partnership with. It is highly probable that our American term came from the French *cahute,* a small hut or cabin, or the related Dutch *kajuit* of the same meaning. The connecting link has not yet been found—the use, that is, of a French or Dutch expression which our great-grandparents adopted—but the kind of partnership or league-ship indicated by "in cahoots with" is obviously that which would be expected of the fellow inhabitants of a small cabin, of men closely engaged in a joint undertaking. The expression dates at least from the early nineteenth century, if not back to the Revolution.

to go to the dogs

Sometimes things are thrown to the dogs or sent to the dogs, but nowadays, at least, it is usually the country or the younger generation that is going to the dogs. In any case, "to the dogs" means utter ruin, straight to hell, the demnition bow-wows. The dog, you see, was not always the house pet that it has now largely become. It was kept for its utility, chiefly in hunting. Such food as it received from its master might be no more than the bones tossed over his shoulder into the straw litter that covered the floor. Our first record of the figurative usage is in Thomas Cooper's *Dictionary* (1563), rightly named *Thesaurus Linguae Romanae et Britannicae,* in the Latin phrase: *addicere aliquem canibus,* to bequeath him to dogs.

to lock the barn (or stable) door after the horse is stolen

To take out automobile insurance after your car has been stolen, or after you've had an accident; to take belated precautions, especially on one's property. Apperson reports that the Romans had the same idea: as quoted from Plautus's *Asinaria,* he gives: *Ne post tempus prædæ præsidium parem* (After the time of plunder one provides protection). But the English aphorism is also very old. We find it in John Gower's *Confessio amantis* (1390): "For whan the grete Stiede Is stole, thanne he [Negligence] taketh hiede, and maketh the stable dore fast." And the saying has come down through the years. We in America are more likely to say "barn door" rather than "stable door," though we recognize either term.

not to know if one is afoot or on horseback

To be so completely confused, thoroughly upset, or beside oneself as to be unable to determine whether one is walking or riding; to be utterly befuddled. This degree of pixilation, or this way of expressing it, is apparently known only in America; at least the saying originated here. In literary usage it has been traced only as far back as 1895, in the *Century Magazine* of that year—"Sam he had a keg hat on, all shiny silk, and a red necktie thet Car' Jane hed made him git, and he didn't know whether he was afoot or a-hossback." But undoubtedly the saying was in fairly common use in some sections of the country many, many years before that. Both of my parents, born in the early 1850's in central Ohio, used it so familiarly as to indicate early acquaintance with it, as if from their own parents or grandparents.

talking through one's hat

To talk nonsense; to indulge in fanciful dreams. Just how this expression came into everyday American speech is now a mystery. From the printed evidence it's not very old, as expressions go; probably no more than seventy years. But what event or circumstance brought it into the language? Because of the date of the earliest record, and the medium in which it appeared—*The World,* New York, May 13, 1888—the notion persisted in my mind for several years that it had a political significance. It was at about that time that Benjamin Harrison's friends were advocating that he be the Republican nominee for the presidency at the forthcoming convention. One of Harrison's foibles was the beautiful tall beaver hat that he affected. It became his natural dignity, but later cartoonists, especially those on opposition papers, such as *The World,* made much of it, showing the president as almost overwhelmed by a prodigious beaver hat. But, alas, it was no cartoonist who coined the expression, and it was not Benjamin Harrison who was first said to be "talking through his hat." The phrase that appeared in *The World* was in an unsigned article entitled "How About White Shirts?" which dealt with a prosaic discussion of the fact that drivers and conductors of street cars in New York wore white shirts, although those in Chicago did not. The phrase was merely part of the conversation of a New York driver with the reporter. He was quoted as saying, in part, "Dis is only a bluff dey're makin' —see! Dey're talkin' tru deir hats." And since the driver did not have to explain his meaning to the reporter, nor the reporter to the readers of *The World,* it is certain that "talking through one's hat" was a familiar expression in 1888, at least in New York.

all wool and a yard wide

Of top quality, character, or the like; absolutely genuine; the real McCoy; fine in every respect; as, Knute Rockne was regarded

196 ·

by all who knew him as all wool and a yard wide. Fraudulence and deceit in the manufacture and sale of woolen cloth were practiced in England certainly as long ago as the reign of Edward IV, according to an act of 1464 against such practices. Further acts of 1483 and 1515 and even to the time of George III, however, indicate that, after a brief flurry, the laws were quietly disregarded until dishonesty again became too flagrant. An act in the short reign of Edward VI is specific, asserting that some clothiers "do daylie more and more studdye rather to make monye then to make good cloths . . . and doe daylie . . . practyse sleight and slender makinge, some by myngelinge of yernes of diverse spynnynges in one clothe, some by myngelinge Fell Wool and Lambes Wooll with Fleese. . . . some by overstretchinge them upon the tenter . . . fynallye by usinge so manye subtill sleights and untruithes as when the clothes soe made be put in the water to trye them, they ryse out of the same neither in lengthe nor bredeth as they ought to doe."

In America, as long as wool was spun and woven in the home for home consumption, it was honestly made, but when itinerant merchants began to travel around the countryside selling cloth from New England mills, their products were not always as represented. To bolster sales they began to adopt the slogan, "all wool and a yard wide," thus proclaiming, with tongue in cheek perhaps, that the cloth contained no shoddy or other adulterant and that it was full width. By the 1880's this slogan had passed into the language in its current meaning. The first it appeared in print was in *Peck's Sunshine* (1882), by George W. Peck, the author of *Peck's Bad Boy,* a favorite possession of my youth.

Ivy League

This Ivy label, in words of Leo Riordan in *The Saturday Evening Post,* November 7, 1953, "was an apt designation coined by a sports-writer to characterize old-line institutions." It refers specifically to the football teams of the colleges, Yale, Harvard, Princeton, Dartmouth, Brown, Cornell, Columbia, and University of Pennsylvania. The sportswriter to whom Riordan referred was Caswell Adams, now of the New York *Journal American.* In a letter to me, which I am privileged to quote, Adams thus described the episode:

It is true that, rather unconsciously, I did coin the phrase back in the mid-thirties. If I remember correctly, it was when Fordham's football team was riding high and playing big-name teams from all over the country. One afternoon mention in the office was made of Columbia and Princeton and the like and I, with complete humorous disparagement in mind, said, "Oh they're just Ivy League." Stanley Woodward, then sports editor of the New York *Herald Tribune* [with which Adams was then connected] picked up the phrase the next day and credited me with it.

But Mr. Adams does not mention the fact that, like "Main Line," the phrase is now sometimes used, also with humorous or even slightly sardonic disparagement, to designate institutions or, especially, literary groups which consider themselves somewhat superior to the rest of us.

like a bat out of hell

Moving or speaking, etc., with extreme speed; like greased lightning; hell-bent for election. Though this might have become a part  of British aviation slang in the First World War, as Partridge says in his *Dictionary of Slang and Unconventional English* (1953 edition), it was certainly in use in the United States at least by the turn of the century—and, I suspect, ten or twenty years earlier than that. It was familiar to my ears in my college days in Colorado, back in 1903–04. A possible explanation of source of origin is that because bats shun the light, they would be in great haste to escape from the incandescent flames of the lower regions.

Back Bay

A fashionable residential district of Boston, Massachusetts. Formerly this was a basin of the Charles River, an inner harbor of Boston. From 1856 it was gradually drained and filled in and laid out in fine wide streets, including Commonwealth Avenue, one of the finest boulevards in America. Hence, used attributively, representative of the culture, thought, accent, etc., of Boston.

flat on one's back

Helpless; without further recourse; at the end of one's rope. Although usually employed in a figurative sense, the original meaning was literal. One who is actually flat on his back is so completely disabled through sickness or injury as to be helpless, unable to fend for himself. Figuratively, the meaning may indicate helplessness through lack of power or through lack of financial means.

to back water

Literally, this was said of a ship, boat, canoe, or the like, to which the paddle wheel was reversed, or the oars or paddles were moved backward. Hence, figuratively, one is said to back water when obliged to retract a statement or reverse a position or withdraw from a situation. The expression dates from the early days of the steamboat, the early nineteenth century.

fifth columnist

This expression was wrongly attributed in *A Hog on Ice* to the Spanish general, Emilio Mola. It should have been credited to Lieutenant General Queipo de Llano, famous as the "broadcasting general" during the Spanish Civil War. In 1936, in the early days of the war, broadcasting to the Loyalist forces in Madrid he threatened, "We have four columns on the battlefield against you and a fifth column inside your ranks." This was the first recognition in modern warfare of organized forces behind the battle lines ready to sabotage the defense of a position.

brain trust

A group of experts; especially, a group organized to aid in the shaping of policies, etc.; hence, derisively, any group of advisers. The term was first coined by James M. Kieran, a reporter for *The New York Times*. It had been announced at Hyde Park that Franklin D. Roosevelt, the Democratic candidate for the presidency in 1932, was preparing a series of campaign speeches and that the services of three Columbia University professors—Rexford G. Tugwell, Raymond Moley, and Adolf A. Berle, Jr.—had been engaged to assist, as experts in economics and political science. Kieran tried unsuccessfully to label this group the "Brains Trust," in his articles for *The Times,* but it was not until after Roosevelt took office and other reporters had adopted the term for the augmented group of non-political advisers which the president retained that it became generally used, now reduced to "brain trust." The first printed use was apparently in *Newsweek,* September 2, 1933: "The President's Brain Trust, a little band of intellectuals, sat at the center of action as similar bands have done in revolutions of the past."

African dominoes (or golf)

Popular names for the game of craps, a gambling game played with a pair of dice. The game is especially favored among American Negroes, hence, "African"; the term "dominoes" alludes to the combined number of pips on the two dice, identical with those on the face of dominoes. "Golf" is in ironical reference to the usual financial status of the players and to the great disparity in the comparative cost of equipment.

asleep at the switch

Unprepared; lacking alertness; inattentive. Undoubtedly this American expression was originally railway terminology and was almost literal in meaning. It dates from the time when railroad switches or turnouts were thrown or turned by levers operated by hand, either by switch-tenders or brakemen. In a freight yard especially, where it was the duty of the switch-tender to shunt cars to the proper tracks, alertness was an essential. Lack of attention gave rise to the charge that he was "asleep at the switch."

right down (or up) one's alley

Peculiarly adapted to one's ability or talent, or particularly attractive to one: "By virtue of his knowledge of Greek and Latin, work on a dictionary was right down Phil's alley"; "That ad for a

200 ·

young man to drive a car to Mexico was right up my alley." It has been suggested, learnedly, that these expressions may have originated from baseball, from the fact that "down the alley" means a ball so hit as to go between the fielders, usually good for a home run. But I am inclined to think that "alley," in these phrases, is merely a substitute for "street," or the locality on which one lives, that "right down (or up) my alley" is merely a figurative way of saying "right in the locality (or specialty) in which I am most at home, or most familiar."

to have hold of the wrong end of the stick

To have the wrong slant; to have another guess coming; to be misinformed, or to misinterpret a story. The *stick* was originally a *staff,* and he who had "the worse end of the staff," as was the saying in the sixteenth century, was on the receiving end of a bout  with quarter-staves, those six- to eight-foot rods made familiar to us through the tales of Robin Hood and his merry band. Obviously, the one on the receiving end was getting the punishment, which accounts for the former and still occasional meaning of the phrase, to be at a disadvantage. And also obviously, the one being worsted in such a combat must confess that he is in the wrong, which accounts for the meaning of our present saying. Curiously, however, no instance of this current saying has been found earlier than the late nineteenth century.

alley cat

Any homeless or stray cat, especially one frequenting alleys in search of food in garbage cans, etc. By extension, a prostitute or a street-walker furtively seeking customers.

to get the drop on (a person)

To have a marked advantage; literally, to have a person covered with a gun before that person is able to draw his own weapon.

According to Mary A. Jackson's *Memoirs of Stonewall Jackson* (1895), this phrase originated during the War between the States. At least, she wrote: "They had seventy-three pieces of artillery, one battery being siege guns or thirty pounder Parrotts, but the elevated position of McLaws and Walker gave them decidedly the drop, not only on the big guns but on the whole Federal line." Nevertheless, long before her *Memoirs* were written, back in 1869 in fact, the traveler, Alexander K. McClure, wrote in his *Three Thousand Miles through the Rocky Mountains:* "So expert is he with his faithful pistol, that the most scientific of rogues have repeatedly attempted in vain to get 'the drop' on him." And, for that matter, I think it most likely that the literal phrase was in use during the famous days of the Forty-Niners, or possibly much earlier.

a Donnybrook fair

Strife and contention; a melee; Bedlam broke loose; hell's a-popping. Why? Because Donnybrook, now a part of Dublin, was a place where, every year for six centuries beginning in 1204, a riotous fair was held each August. Originally the fair lasted for two weeks, but eventually that became too taxing for even the most fun-loving of the natives of the town and the exhibitions and festivities were cut down in later years to one week. Needless to say, huge quantities of usquebaugh were consumed even in that one week, and a quick-tempered Irishman found ample occasion to crack a crown with his stout shillelah. Probably to the regret of none, the fair was discontinued in 1885.

Philadelphia lawyer

An astute person; sometimes one whose cleverness leads him into shady practices. In my explanation of this phrase in *A Hog on Ice* the account of its origin as given by the historian John Fiske was accidentally omitted, as I was reminded by a correspondent.

According to Fiske, the expression stems from the noted trial of John Peter Zenger in 1735. Zenger, a New York printer, began to publish a newspaper, the New York *Weekly Journal* in 1733, which became the organ of the popular party in that colony. Attacks upon the administration of the governor of the colony, William Cosby,

202 ·

brought about the arrest of Zenger on a charge of libel, and he was held in jail, awaiting trial, for about eight months. Friends busied themselves in his behalf and eventually secured the services of Andrew Hamilton, former Attorney General of Philadelphia. At the trial Hamilton admitted the publication of the statements charged by the prosecution, but maintained that inasmuch as the statements were true no libel had been committed. The jury supported that contention and gave a verdict of not guilty, thus establishing the principle of freedom of the press in America. Thus Fiske reports, people then proclaimed, "It took a Philadelphia lawyer to get Zenger out."

Fiske's statement may be true, but, regrettably, no proof has yet been discovered that people in New York or elsewhere had actually made such a remark. Nevertheless the expression was certainly in use before 1788. In that year, as found by Allen Walker Read, the *Columbian Magazine* of Philadelphia printed a "Letter from a Citizen of America," "written in London," to his "Correspondent in Philadelphia," a portion of which reads, "They have a proverb here [London], which I do not know how to account for;—in speaking of a difficult point, they say, it would puzzle a Philadelphia lawyer."

But there are other accounts. One credits it to an unnamed attorney in colonial days who rescued two British sailors from some unnamed difficulty they experienced in the City of Brotherly Love. Again, it is reported that there was a saying in New England that any three Philadelphia lawyers were a match for the devil, though I have found no proof of that report—nor substantiation of the statement.

to know where the shoe pinches

Though the Romans of old said *calceus urit,* they meant it physically—the shoe or sandal frets or pinches. However, the figurative sense—where hardship occurs or difficulty lies or trouble may be experienced—has been in English usage for at least six centuries. Chaucer had it in *Canterbury Tales* (*c.* 1386) when, in "The Merchant's Tale," he has the merchant's brother say:

> ". . . Myn neighebours aboute
> Sayn that I have the moste stedefast wyf,
> And eek the meekest oon that berith lyf;
> But I woot best [know best], wher wryngith [pinches] me my scho."

The French phrase, a direct transalation, is *c'est là que le soulier me pince,* though *c'est là que le bât me blesse,* literally, "that's where the saddle galls me," is heard more frequently. Germans say, *wissen wo einen der Schuh druckt,* "to know where the shoe pinches one." Spaniards say, *Cada uno sabe donde le aprieta el zapato,* "Each one knows where the shoe pinches him."

absent treatment

In the United States this expression is used with two differing meanings. Originally, and properly, it is a term in Christian Science for a treatment by a healer given at the request of and for the benefit of an absent person. But the term has also acquired a slang sense: treatment such as that shown to a person or an animal not present. One gives a child, a dog, another person the absent treatment by speaking of him or it as if he were non-existent or not within hearing distance, though actually the speaker knows him to be present and able to hear what is said.

the devil to pay

Serious difficulty; great trouble or misfortune; perplexity; confusion; mishap. "There'll be the devil to pay if I don't get home in time for dinner." There are two schools of thought about the original meaning of this. One is that it related to witchcraft, to the selling of one's soul to the devil and the payment exacted for its release. This would seem to be the sense in the earliest quotation that we have, occurring under date of approximately 1400 in the poem, "Titivillus," in the collection of ancient manuscripts, *Reliquiæ Antiquæ*—"Beit wer be at tome for ay, Than her to serve the devil to pay."

But "devil" is also a nautical term for the seam nearest the keel of a vessel, and "pay" means to calk. Hence, among sailors "the devil to pay" could mean to calk the seam nearest the keel. This could be done, in former days, only when the vessel had been careened, tipped on its side. Such an operation, between tides, would be difficult, especially so if the expanded form of the expression is considered—"the devil to pay and no pitch hot," as we find it in Sir Walter Scott's *The Pirate* (1821): "If they hurt but one hair of Cleveland's head, there will be the devil to pay, and no pitch hot." Proof is lacking that the nautical was the original sense, but this is the logical source of the phrase.

tooth and nail

Yes, it means exactly what cute little Mary Ann means when she goes after her pestiferous older small brother who is torturing her

dolly. She bites and digs in with her nails. And she and her ancestors before her, both sides of the family, have been using those natural weapons of offense and defense since Noah was a pup. Thus *with tooth and nail* long ago became an English phrase signifying "with all the powers at one's command." The old Latin equivalent was *toto corpore atque omnibus ungulis,* "with all the body and every nail." In France, it's *bec et ongles,* closely approaching our English phrase, but with the literal meaning, "beak and talons."

to the bitter end

To the last extremity; to death or utter defeat. This expression has a double meaning, but it is hardly likely that the poetic resemblance between the two meanings is anything more than chance. That is, in the words of the famous Captain John Smith in his *A Sea Grammar* (1627): "A Bitter is but the turne of a Cable about the Bits, and veare it out [let it out] by little and little. And the Bitters end is that part of the Cable doth stay within boord." Or, as a later seaman put it, "When a chain or rope is paid out to the bitter-end, no more remains to be let go"—when the end of the chain or rope reaches the bitts, obviously no more can be paid out. But death, the end of life, has long been thought to be bitter, and it is no more than natural that, poetically, we should say that when one has come to the end of life, the "end of one's rope," that he has come "to the bitter end." (It has been contended that nautical usage is, properly, "to the better end," the end of the rope or chain which, being inboard, is little used. But the language of the sea does not substantiate this argument.)

loaded for bear

To be fully prepared for any contingency; to be well prepared; hence, ready to fly into a rage. Originally this had a hunting significance; the bear, being the largest of dangerous American wild animals and likely to be encountered in any region of wild game, a hunter did not regard himself as prepared unless his gun carried a charge heavy enough to kill a bear. Undoubtedly, use of the expression—often written and spoken, "loaded for b'ar"—goes back to the days when the West was wild and woolly, but evidence of this has not yet been turned up in our literature. Modern slang has introduced a new meaning into the phrase—to be well loaded; spifflicated; drunk as a boiled owl.

blowing one's top

Possibly the "top" in this expression alluded originally to the top of a volcano, which would be shot into a thousand pieces with a tremendous noise during a violent explosion and scattered over the neighborhood with a devastating effect. "Blow," at least, has been used in the sense of "to erupt; to go to pieces by explosion" for several centuries. Much the same effect occurs when, in modern slang, a person "blows his top." He lets off steam in a violent explosion of temper; he shouts; he cares not a whit where or upon whom the pieces may fall. In short, he gets furious with rage. The expression is also used in a far milder sense: a crazy person, that is, or a person who is befuddled by drink and acts brainless is now sometimes said to have blown his top.

to bleed one white

Literally, this is to cause one to lose so much blood that he becomes pale, but for the past three hundred years men have been

206 ·

said to "bleed" when they have unwillingly or through fraud parted with an undue sum of money, as through blackmail or the like. When the victim has been "bled white," in modern parlance, he has paid through the nose to such an extent that the extortionist sees that his racket has come to an end.

not worth a rap

Having no intrinsic value; not worth a straw, nor a tinker's dam, nor beans. We don't know just how *rap* got its name, but it was a very small coin which, though not legal tender, was passed for a halfpence in Ireland during the early eighteenth century. It was because of the lack of legal small currency and in protest against a lopsided patent issued to one William Wood by George I for the coinage of copper halfpence in Ireland that Dean Jonathan Swift wrote the celebrated *Drapier Letters* in 1724. Concerning the *rap*, he wrote in one of the letters, "Copper halfpence or farthings . . . have been for some time very scarce, and many counterfeits passed about under the name of raps."

And when we say, "I don't care a rap," it is the same worthless coin to which we refer.

fourth estate

The newspaper press as a distinct power in the state, from the license it exercises, the liberties it enjoys, or the power it wields. (The first three estates, as ultimately represented in the British Parliament, are the Lords Spiritual, the Lords Temporal, and the Commons.)

Thomas Carlyle, in *Heroes and Hero Worship* (1841), credited the expression in this sense to the statesman, Edmund Burke— "Burke said there were three Estates in Parliament, but, in the Reporters' gallery yonder, there sat a Fourth Estate more important far than they all"—but the statement is not recorded anywhere in Burke's published works. Moreover, in the *Edinburgh Review* in 1826, Thomas Macaulay used the phrase in an essay on Henry Hallam's *Constitutional History*, in the eighth paragraph from the end: "The gallery in which the reporters sit has become a *fourth estate* of the realm." As Carlyle himself was a Scottish reviewer and wrote for the *Edinburgh Review,* it is probable that he attributed the thought to the wrong author.

In strict justice, however, the novelist, Henry Fielding, should receive some of the credit. Seventy-six years earlier, writing for the *Covent-Garden Journal,* he said: "None of our political writers . . . take notice of any more than three estates, namely, Kings, Lords, and Commons . . . passing by in silence that very large and powerful body which form the *fourth estate* in this community . . . The Mob." And, though erroneously, Lord Lucius Cary Falkland has been similarly credited. While Richard Cromwell was Lord Protector of England, according to Charles Knight's *Popular History of England,* Lord Falkland, in the course of a speech in 1660 in Parliament, said: "You have been a long time talking of the three estates; there is a *fourth* which, if not well looked to, will turn us all out of doors"—referring to the army. The army did ultimately turn Cromwell out, but Falkland made no such speech —he died sixteen years before Cromwell's short-lived tenure of the office his brilliant father, Oliver, had created.

to go by the board

"Board," in nautical language, is the side of a ship. Thus "overboard," for example, means over the side of a ship; hence, out of the ship, into the sea, and "by the board" has the same meaning— i.e., down the ship's side, overboard. Accordingly, "to go by the board," in its literal sense, is to go down the ship's side, to fall overboard and to be carried away; hence, to be lost for good. These several literal meanings date back at least three centuries, and some are older. But the figurative sense of our present phrase—meaning, to be utterly lost, as if carried away by the sea—is scarcely more than a hundred years old. The earliest literary usage thus reported occurs in *The Autobiography of a Beggar Boy* (1855) by James D. Burn: "Every instinct and feeling of humanity goes by the board."

to leave no stone unturned

To use every expedient at one's command. Some say that this was the reply given by the Delphic oracle when Polycrates, the

Theban general, asked for aid in discovering the treasures said to have been buried by the slain leader of the defeated Persian army, Mardonius, before the battle of Plataea, 479 B.C. Actually, according to the historian Herodotus, the answer of the oracle is usually translated, "to leave no stone unturned," by which was meant, "to move all things." The English saying arose sometime in the first half of the sixteenth century and could have been common before that to indicate any exhaustive search, as for some valued object lost in the destruction of a baronial hall or the like. The earliest mention in print is in *A Manifest Detection of the Most Vyle and Detestable Use of Dice-play* (*c.* 1550): "He wil refuse no labor nor leaue no stone vnturned, to pick vp a penny." Probably this was at first a variation of the older "to leave no straw unturned," which, with the straw-littered and dust-covered floors of the Middle Ages, meant an even more exhaustive search than among stones.

talking to one like a Dutch uncle

In *A Hog on Ice* I expressed the opinion that the concept of a severe reprimand from an uncle of Dutch ancestry appeared to be American. Though I have nothing to offer to contradict that opinion, I have run across literary instances which indicate that the original of such an uncle was Roman. The poet Horace, that is, living in the first century B.C., twice referred to the tongue-lashings of an uncle. In the *Satires,* II, 3, is the line, *Ne sis patruus mihi,* which may be translated, "Do not play the uncle over me," and in the later *Odes,* III, 12, is the more positive, *Metuentes patruæ verbera linguæ,* "Fearing the tongue-lashings of an uncle."

baby-kisser

An aspirant for public office who attempts to win the favor of parents by a show of affection toward their children. Probably the Greeks and Romans had a word for this also, for the politicians of ancient days certainly practiced all the other arts known to modern office-seekers. Especially in Rome in the time of the republic. Here the *ambitor,* literally he who went around (seeking votes), resorted to every known expedient of that day to influence voters in his favor, even in the face of stringent laws against bribery and corruption, so if the kissing of babies and the patting of small boys on the head would ingratiate him, he could not have missed such a chance. The first application of the American term appears to have been in the presidential campaign of 1884 when General Benjamin F. Butler, disaffected with the Democratic nomination of Grover Cleveland, ran on an independent Greenback-Labor ticket. In the election, however, against Cleveland, Democrat, and Blaine, Republican, Butler was an also-ran. As the Cincinnati *Times-Star* put it, "As a baby-kisser, Ben Butler is not a success."

all quiet on the Potomac

Peaceful; undisturbed; a time of ease or quiet enjoyment: from the frequent repetition of the phrase in bulletins issued during the War between the States, 1861–1865. The original expression has been ascribed to General George B. McClellan (1826–85), who was in command of the Army of the Potomac in 1861 and 1862, but who received much criticism in Washington because of alleged dilatory policies and lack of aggressiveness. The phrase sometimes appears as "all quiet *along* the Potomac," from the poem, "The Picket Guard" (1861), by Ethel Lynn Beers, the sixth stanza of which is—

> All quiet along the Potomac tonight,
>   No sound save the rush of the river,
> While soft falls the dew on the face of the dead—
>   The picket's off duty forever.

to get ahead, to be ahead (of the game), to come out ahead

We, in America, use the first expression in two differing ways. Thus when we say, "Jeff is getting ahead in the store he has recently opened," we mean that Jeff is prospering, is on the way toward a successful venture. But when we say, "Maggie Jones has thought up a new scheme to get ahead of conceited Mary Smith," we mean that Maggie is contriving to surpass, or outdo, or outwit Madam Smith.

"To be ahead" and "to come out ahead" also carry the thought of financial gain, of having more than one started with, the converse of "to be behind." Such is the meaning in "He was ahead on the deal with Aaron, but he got behind when he began to trade with Simon." This idiom is often expanded into "to be ahead of the game," because business transactions so often present the aspects of gambling; as, "When I sold the business I was twenty thousand dollars ahead of the game." And when we say, "The women came out ahead on the church bazaar," we mean that they did well, or at least that the financial gain was greater than the cost.

to give the air to (a person)

To tie the can to; to fire; to dismiss; to discharge from employment; literally, to put out of doors. A British counterpart of this modern American slang is "to give one the sack" (see *A Hog on Ice*). The expression also has a negative meaning in the language of love. When Joan gives the air to John, she terminates a courtship by giving John to understand definitely and unmistakably that his attentions are unwanted, or she breaks off an acquaintance before John can begin to get romantic notions.

eager beaver

A person who is always "rarin' to go," eager to start at whatever is to be done. Undoubtedly the term developed naturally from one who "works like a beaver," one who works rapidly and assiduously. It bears no relation to the "beaver" or full beard worn by some men. This latter term was transferred from ancient helmets, from the movable part of the helmet covering the chin, called "beaver" from Old French *bavière,* a bib. Let me add, before I'm accused of missing a point, that the modern "eager beaver" is usually so overly zealous as to attempt duties that do not concern him, and thus he becomes an obnoxious character, one thoroughly disliked by his associates.

INDEX

A 1, 24
absent treatment, 204
according to one's lights, 64
ace in the hole, 171
actor, ham, 43
adder, deaf as an, 39–40
admirable Crichton, 29–30
ado, to make much, about nothing, 22
afoot, not to know if one is, or on horseback, 195–96
African dominoes (golf), 200
ahead, to get (be, come out), 210–11
air, castle in the, 168
air, to give the, to (a person), 167, 211
air, to go up in the, 83
air, to make the, blue, 117–18
alive and kicking, to be, 124
alley, right down (up) one's, 200–1
alley cat, 201
alpha and omega, 177
also-ran, 169–70
ambulance chaser, 177
ans, no ifs, nor buts, 48
Anthony (Antony) over, 181–82
A-number-one, 24
anvil chorus, 41
apron strings, tied to one's mother's (wife's), 191
aristocracy, codfish, 173
arm, a shot in the, 57
arm, to talk one's, off, 119
asleep at the switch, 38, 200
ax, to get it where the chicken got the, 138, 146

B, not to know, from a battledore (broomstick, bull's foot, buffalo's foot), 188–89

baby act, to do (put on, pull, play) the, 155
baby act, to plead the, 155
baby-kisser, 209–10
back and fill, 32
Back Bay, 198–99
back seat, to take a, 182–83
back-seat driver, 182–83
back to the wall, with one's, 97
back water, 199
badger game, 176–77
bag, to hold the, 108–9
bait, to fish or cut, 130–31
ball, to carry the, 49
ball, to keep one's eye on the, 124
ball, to keep the, rolling, 147
ball, to play, with one, 101
banquet, Barmecide, 92
banquet, Lucullian, 55
bark, to take the, off, 193–94
bark, to talk the, off a tree, 193–94
Barmecide feast (banquet), 92
barn door, to lock the, after the horse is stolen, 195
barrel, over a, 133
barrelhead, cash on the, 118
base, off one's, 121
bat out of hell, like a, 60, 198
battledore, not to know B from a, 188–89
beans, full of, 54–55
beans, not worth a hill of, 33, 207
bear, loaded for, 206
beard of the prophet, by the, 123
bear with a sore head, like a, 144–45
beat the living daylights out of one, 115
beaver, a gone, 90
beaver, eager, 211

beaver, to work like a, 211
behind the 8-ball, 75, 123
bell, to ring a, 129
belt, hitting below the, 161
Betsy, Heavens to, ix–xi
Betsy, I declare to, 43–44
between the devil and the deep blue sea, 32
billy goat, playing horse with a, 172–73
bite, to put the, on one, 191–92
bite off more than one can chew, 41, 53
bite the dust (ground, sand), 84
bite the thumb at, 190–91
bitter end, to the, 205–6
black-coated worker, 29
bleed one white, 206–7
bloody ground, dark and, 37–38
blow for a blow, 90
blowing one's top, 206
blow one's own nose, 124
blue, to make the air, 117–18
blue streak, like a, 60
blue streak, to talk a, 119
board, to go by the, 208
boat, to be in the same, 98
boats, to burn one's, 160
bobtail, rag-tag and, 57
boiling, to keep the pot, 147–48
boner, to pull a, 73
bones, to make no, about, 30
bone, to pick, 24–25
book, to take a leaf out of one's, 136
book, to throw the, at one, 157
bootstraps, lift (raise, hoist, pull up) oneself by his, xi–xii, 51–53
bosom, to nourish a viper (snake) in one's, 111
bounce, to get (be given) the, 163
box the compass, 47
brain trust, 199–200
brass, to double in, 166
bread and butter, to quarrel with one's, 75
breakfast, from hell to, 126–27
bridges, to burn one's, 160
broomstick, not to know B from a, 188–89
bucket, a drop in the, 96–97

buffalo's foot, not to know B from a, 188–89
bug in a rug, snug as a, 31
bug's ear, cute as a, 30–31
bull, to shoot the, 181
bull session, 181
bull's-eye, to hit the, 137
bull's foot, not to know B from a, 188–89
bump on a log, like a, 33, 115–16
burn one's boats (bridges), 160
bury the hatchet (tomahawk), 183–84
bushel, to hide one's light under a, 135–36
busman's holiday, 192
buts, no ifs, ans, nor, 48
butter-and-egg man (big), 179–80
buttons, minus some, 94

Cadmean victory, 193
cahoots, in, with (one), 194
Cain, to raise, 73
cake, one's is dough, 27
calf, fatted, to kill the, 194
call off the dogs, 124
call the turn, 27–28
camel, to strain at a gnat and swallow a, 139–40
can, to tie the, to one, 167–68, 211
canoe, to paddle one's own, 124
cap, to set one's, at (for) a person, 188
capers, to cut, 170
card, to speak by the, 27
carpet, on the, 62, 146
carry the ball, 49
cash in one's checks (chips), 28
cash on the barrelhead, 118
cash on the counter, 118
casting pearls before swine, 147
castle in the air (in Spain), 168
cat, alley, 201
cat and mouse, to play, with one, 21
cats and dogs, raining, 184
cat's-paw, to be made a, 162
caught flat-footed, 38
Cerberus, a sop to, 125
chalk, not for money, marbles, nor, 70

hammer, to bring (put) under the, 139
hammer and tongs, 177
hand, high, with a, 121
hand in one's checks (chips), 28
handsaw, not to know a hawk from a, 189
handwriting on the wall, 87
hang by a thread, 176
hanged, drawn, and quartered, 50
hang on by the eyelashes, 53
harp on one string, 122
hat, old, 127
hat, talking through one's, 196
hat, to eat one's, 184–85
hatband, as queer (tight) as Dick's, 168–69
hatchet, to bury the, 183–84
hatter, mad as a, 88–89
hawk, not to know a, from a handsaw, 189
hay, to make, while the sun shines, 102
haywire, gone, 56, 94
head, neither, nor tail, 79
head, sore, like a bear with a, 144–45
head, to hit the nail on the, 137–38
head, to knock one's, against a wall, 61
head or heels, not to know if on, 32
heart, to cross one's, 127
heart, to warm the cockles of one's, 91
heat, to turn the, on, 122
heaven, in seventh, 106–7
Heavens to Betsy, ix–xi
heeled, to be well, 86
heels, down at the, 86
hell, go to, 40
hell, like a bat out of, 60, 198
hell-bent for election, 198
hell on wheels, 166
hell or high water, come (in spite of), 129–30
hell to breakfast, 126–27
hem and haw, 32, 98–99
hemlock, gosh all, 91
hen, wet, mad as a, 126
hen's teeth, as scarce as (scarcer than), 126

herring, dead as a, 38–39
het up, to get, 45
hide, hair and, 145
hide one's light under a bushel, 135–36
hiding, to give one a, 193
high horse, to pull one off his, 78
high jinks, 70–71
Hill, Sam, 93
hill, to go over the, 77
hill of beans, not worth a, 33
hinges, off his, 94
hit the bull's-eye, 137
hit the nail on the head, 137–38
hitting below the belt, 161
hob, to raise (play), 73–74
hocus-pocus, 85
hoe, a long (hard) row to, 125
hoe one's own row, 124
hog, root, or die, 58
Hogan's goat, like, 88
hog wild, to go, 45
hoist with one's own petard, 77
hold your horses, 145–46
hole, ace in the, 171
hole, to be in a, 97
holiday, busman's, 192
home, nothing to write, about, 108
hook or by crook, 153–54
hops, as mad (thick, fast) as, 68–69
horn, to blow one's own, 117
horns, hair and hide, and tallow, 145
horn spoon, by the great, 123–24
horse, a gone, 90
horse, dead, paying (working) for a, 154–55
horse, dead, to flog a, 155
horse, playing, with a billy goat, 172–73
horseback, not to know if one is afoot or on, 195–96
horseleech, the daughter of the, 156
horses, hold your, 145–46
hot, to make it, for, 122
hot, to strike while the iron is, 23–24, 102
hot dog, 152–53
hour, at the eleventh, 21–22
how-de-do, in a pretty, 123, 128
Hubert, Sir, praise from, 46

humble pie, to eat, 184
hunkydory, 93
hurrah's nest, 74–75

ice, thin, to skate over (on), 149–50
ice, to break the, 77
ifs, ans, nor buts, no, 48
Indian giver, 103–4
Indian sign, 95
injury, to add insult to, 83
insult, to add, to injury, 83
iron, to strike while the, is hot, 23–24, 102
iron curtain, 189–90
irons, to have many (too many) in the fire, 53–54
ish kabibble, 81
itching palm (tongue, ear, foot), 146
ivory tower, 131–32
Ivy League, 197–98

Jehoshaphat, great jumping, 123
jib, to dislike (like) the cut of one's, 80
Jim Crow, to jump, 134–35
jinks, high, 70–71
Johnny-come-lately, 59–60
joint, to put (have) one's nose out of, 174–75
Jones, Davy's, locker, 158
Joneses, keeping up with the, 141–42
jowl, cheek by, 30
Juba, to dance, 60
jump Jim Crow, 134–35

keeping up with the Joneses, 141–42
kettle of fish, in a pretty, 123
kibosh, on the, 56
kick, to get a, out of, 71
kick against the pricks, 61
kicking, to be alive, and, 124
kill the fatted calf, 194
kitty, to fatten (sweeten) the, 135
knees of the gods, 80
knock one's head against a wall, 61
knock on wood, 96
knock the spots off one, 102–3
know chalk from cheese, 31–32

lam, to take it on the, 77

lame duck, 42–43
lap of the gods, 80
lares and penates, 66–67
lead by the nose, 31
lead one up (down) the garden (path), 150–51
lead-pipe cinch, 170–71
leaf, to take a, out of one's book, 136
leaf, to turn a new, 61
leap in the dark, 154
leg, to pull one's, 135
legs, with the tail between the, 100
level, on the, 62–63
lick and a promise, 63
lickety-split, 60
lick the stuffing (tar) out of one, 115
lift oneself by his bootstraps, xi–xii, 51–53
light, to hide one's, under a bushel, 135–36
lightning, like greased, 60, 198
lights, according to one's, 64
lily, to paint (gild) the, 54
line, to draw the, 186
linen, dirty, to wash one's, in public, 113–114
lip, to keep a stiff upper, 45, 122
loaded dice, playing with, 50
loaded for bear, 206
lock, stock, and barrel, 75
locker, Davy Jones's, 158
lock the barn (stable) door after the horse is stolen, 195
log, easy as rolling off a, 70
log, like a bump on a, 33, 115–16
loins, to gird (up) one's, 61–62
longbow, drawing a, 192–93
lookout, to keep a sharp, 39
loose, to play fast and, 64
lose one's shirt, 106
love me, love my dog, 48
Lucifer, proud as, 76
Lucullian feast (banquet), 55
lurch, to be left in the, 108–9
lute, a rift in the, 22
lying down, to take (something), 100

tune the old cow died of, 113
turn, to call the, 27–28
turn a new leaf, 61
turn the tables, 138
two-cents' worth, to add one's, 146

uncle, Dutch, talking to one like a, 209
uncle, to say (cry), 112, 133
under the wire, just, 21
up-and-up, on the, 62
up one's alley, 200–1

velvet, on, 112–13
victory, Cadmean, 193
viper, to nourish a, in one's bosom, 111

wagon, water, on the, 84
wait for dead men's shoes, 156
walk the plank, 76
wall, handwriting on the, 87
wall, to go to the, 114
wall, to knock one's head against a, 61
wall, with one's back to the, 97
warm the cockles of one's heart, 91
wash-basin, storm in a, 22
washed up, 182
wash one's dirty linen in public, 113–14
water, a fish out of, 67
water, between wind and, 110
water, cold, to throw, 114
water, high, come (in spite of) hell or, 129–30
water, hot, in, 123

water, to back, 199
water cart (wagon), on the, 84
Waterloo, to meet one's, 114–15
weasel words, 159–60
west, to go, 112
whangdoodle mourneth for his first-born, 111
wheel, to put one's shoulder to the, 106
wheels, hell on, 166
whip, to crack the, 134
whip hand, to have the, 31
whipping boy, 132
whistle, as clean as a, 111–12
white, to bleed one, 206–7
white-collar worker, 29
willing to give one's ears, 160
wind, between, and water, 110
wind, three sheets in the, 81
windmills, to tilt at, 49
wings, to take under one's, 26
win one's spurs, 140
wire, just under the, 21
wolf, to cry, 142
wood, to knock on, 96
wood, unable to see the, for the trees, 152
woodbine, gone where the, twineth, 111
woodpile, a nigger in the, 136, 148
wool, all, and a yard wide, 196–97
wool, to pull the, over one's eyes, 135
working for a dead horse, 154–55
work like a beaver, 211
works, to gum up the, 68
wrack and ruin, to go to, 94